To
Elizabe

THE PREFAB KID

Gregory Holyoake.

Gregory Holyoake

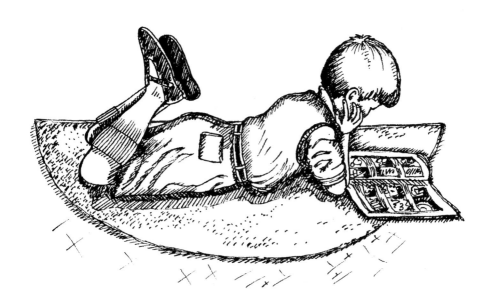

S.B. Publications

First published in 1998 by SB Publications
14 Bishopstone Road, Seaford, East Sussex
Tel: 01323 893498 Email: sbpublications@tiscali.co.uk
Reprinted 2003 and 2009

ISBN 1 85770 175 5

Designed and typeset by JEM Lewes

Illustrations

Anne Churchill
and
Jane Michael

To my best friend
Joy

Down in the jungle,
Living in a tent.
Better than a prefab
– no rent!

Charlie Chester
Stand Easy

CONTENTS

THE PREFAB KID

A FTER the Second World War there was an acute shortage of houses, particularly in south east Kent which, because of the constant bombardment from cross-Channel guns, had earned its reputation as 'Hellfire Corner'. The government solved the problem temporarily by putting up prefabricated homes on bomb sites and scrubland across the country.

Prefabs were detached bungalows built in redundant aircraft factories using aluminium recyled from crashed aeroplanes. They arrived in sections on lorries and were assembled on site in three days, often by prisoners of war. Prefabs, as they were known, were intended to last perhaps ten years but because they were so sturdy whole estates remain in London and the Midlands, although they have entirely disappeared from Kent.

Dad was born into a large family of five sisters and three brothers, in Derby. Before he could embark on any career he was conscripted into the army when war broke out with Germany in 1939. He joined the Royal Artillery and was shipped across the English Channel to fight with the British Expeditionary Force in France.

After the fall of France in 1940 British troops began their strategic withdrawal to the coast at Dunkirk. Prime Minister Winston Churchill ordered all the 'little ships' (everything from a lifeboat to a pleasure steamer) of the south coast to speed across the Channel to the rescue of the stranded troops who were constantly under attack by machine gun fire from enemy planes. Along with thousands of allied soldiers, Dad waded into the water, rifle held aloft, to be picked up and transferred to one of the larger vessels waiting offshore to

8

take them to safety.

Father arrived in Dover where he was offered refreshment before being reunited with his family and regiment. The defeated soldiers had feared recriminations from the local people but they were overwhelmed to find that the whole town had turned out to cheer them as they landed at Admiralty Pier. Miserably, Father had celebrated his 21st birthday while fighting.

Mother, by contrast, had a marvellous war. She enlisted in the WAAF and after her previously sheltered existence she revelled in the plentiful food, travel, excitement and, above all, the companionship of service life. It was while father was stationed on the White Cliffs of Dover, manning a solitary field gun of no certain purpose, that he met Mother when off duty. In due course the couple became engaged.

Towards the end of hostilities Father, who had gone on to fight against the Japanese in India and Burma with the 115th Field regiment, was diagnosed with 'acute fatigue' and shipped home to convalesce. Doctors advised him to look to the future by marrying and raising a family. Thus Sydney married Hilda and raised one son, Gregory, as their sole contribution to the postwar baby boom. Housing was desperately short and, like millions of young newlyweds, they began married life lodging with their in-laws.

Father used to joke that I was born in the USA. By that he meant the Up Stairs Attic of Redan, a reputedly haunted Georgian house in the historic seaside town of Deal in Kent. My grandparents were Morgan Jones, called Pop, a coal miner from Wales, and his wife, Jessie, who hailed from South Yorkshire. Morgan had served in the Welsh Fusiliers during the Great War. Throughout The Second World War the pair worked locally serving troops in the NAAFI where they had been pleasantly surprised by their popularity.

Early in the 1950s my parents were offered a prefab (rent 16 shillings weekly) on an estate two miles inland at Upper Deal. Carter Avenue consisted of twenty or so prefabricated homes in a cul-de-sac crossed by four alleyways one of which led directly into open countryside surrounding the village of Mongeham. Nearby was a spanking new primary school while beyond, across the fields, was the pithead wheel and winding gear of Betteshanger Colliery.

Time now for a fresh start.

Throughout my childhood the war was never mentioned. Toy guns were banned, war films discouraged and even the tin helmets we swapped for jam jars with the rag and bone man were confiscated.

Probably the most violent activity after a dispute among friends was water pistols at dawn. Our gang of 'austerity kids' led a protected, yet tough existence, oblivious to the facts that the cycle shed in the back yard on which we recklessly climbed to play pirates was a resited Anderson shelter and that the

9

trenches still scarring the countryside beyond the allotments where we played
had been abandoned by troops practising for the invasion of D Day.

Almost as soon as my family moved into our prefab – 16 Carter Avenue –
there was a tremendous commotion in the street. A decorated float appeared,
tugged by scouts. Precariously seated on a chair was a lady in a long white
robe, with a cardboard crown, sceptre and orb. Here, it was explained to me,
was Queen Elizabeth II who was about to be crowned in London the next day
(June 2, 1953). I was handed a paper Union Jack which I waved frantically
through the window. For years afterwards I remained truly impressed that the
future Queen of England had deigned to visit our prefabs prior to being

crowned in Westminster Abbey.

There was a street party to celebrate and all the prefabs were decorated with patriotic flags, paper rosettes and cardboard crowns. Red, white and blue. My parents considered me too young to join in these festivities so, held back by reins, I watched though the slats of the garden gate. The occasion gave me a glimpse of my first black person. One of the little girls from the nearby council estate after being dressed in all her finery went to play in the coal bunker. Her mum was highly embarrassed when she presented her sooty child at the party.

At school we were each presented with a china mug and a beaker bearing a

transfer print of the young sovereign. The beaker held my toothbrush until knocked off the bathroom shelf (we daren't tell the Queen!). My coronation mug survives and is considered an antique, but my proudest possession was a model of the coronation coach pulled by eight white horses, made by the famous toy firm Lesney.

Father ran our little home with military precision. A house was something to be proud of: a job was not worth doing unless done properly. Spit and polish . . . rise and shine . . . spick and span . . . The linoleum was polished until slippery, the utility furniture shone, the curtains were changed as regularly as the seasons – a light patterned pair for summer, thick velvet drapes for winter.

The sitting room, which we grandly called the lounge, was the main room. Its low walls were gaily papered – a difficult task since they consisted of large panels held together by vertical metal strips. Decorating a prefab always posed

a problem: did one paper over the bumps or paint the raised strips then wallpaper in between? The focal point was the fireplace. This consisted of a hearth with a stepped mantelpiece covered in mottled beige tiles. Everything was perfectly symmetrical. What you put one side of the fire – candlestick, ashtray, figurine – you balanced on the other. Nothing was ever removed except when dusting was required. All built up towards the eight day striking clock with its irritating Westminster chimes.

Symmetry continued with the furniture. A three-piece suite was obligatory. Two deep leather armchairs were placed either side of the fireplace: Father's under the turned wood lamp standard with its frilly shade; Mother's next to the portable bakelite radio (which we called the wireless). Thrown over the backs were linen anti-macassars to prevent men's greased hair from staining the leather. In the middle, dawn up to the fire in winter, was the matching dull

13

brown settee reserved for visitors who rarely came. Symmetry in our home was, I guess, another result of war. Order after chaos.

There were few ornaments (Dad despised 'knick-knacks') but there was a collection of Wade miniature animals arranged on a zigzag wooden frame fixed to the wall. This was an improvement on the trio of flying ducks or the pair of chalk Alsatians displayed by neighbours. In one corner was a magazine rack holding mother's selection of borrowed women's journals and knitting patterns. 'Knit one, purl one . . .' Stowed to one side was a round leatherette pouffe for me to sit on whenever I could be trusted to keep still.

The fully fitted kitchen was the star attraction of living in a prefab. Along one entire wall was an array of metal cupboards and drawers with hygienic wipe-clean surfaces. There was a neat gas cooker, a fridge and running hot water – amenities that my grandmother, who lived well into the 1970s, never experienced. Washing was still done by hand and always on Mondays. There was a copper to heat extra water and a free standing mangle but no washing machine. Much later mother could afford to hire a 'twin tub', or cycle into the town to use the newly opened laundrette.

It was this kitchen – together with the modern bathroom boasting a complete suite of bath, basin and loo – which made prefabs so desirable.

One day a little girl in the avenue became dangerously ill with a high temperature. The doctor arrived and diagnosed an 'infantile fit'. While he went off in search of a telephone kiosk to call an ambulance the distraught mother called on all her neighbours to collect as many ice cubes as possible from their fridges. The child recovered but the fact that our prefabs were equipped with refrigerators probably saved her life.

Number 16 stood in the centre of a large triangle of land. This was a bonus since few homeowners today possess such an extensive garden. Indeed it was large enough to be divided into several areas: a triangular lawn at the rear where the washing line was strung between two concrete posts; a sizeable vegetable plot at one side and a beautiful rose garden at the front in which Peace, Ena Harkness and Elizabeth of Glamis bloomed beside the crazy paving. Proud dads sent their kids to scoop up precious manure to put around the rose trees whenever a delivery horse visited the avenue.

14

Father spent long hours tending his garden, which attracted the attention of every passer-by. Most admired were the patriotic borders planted with red geraniums, white alyssum and blue lobelia. Inspired at first by Adam the gardener whose strips appeared in the *Daily Express* and later by Percy Thrower's television programme Gardening Club, he was constantly mowing the lawn, feeding the compost heap, creosoting the tool shed and spraying the vegetables with DDT. Once I was given a parcel of land next the rockery where I dutifuly planted my Sutton's seeds then dug them all up the next day to see why they hadn't flowered.

Most summers my wigwam was pitched in the centre of the lawn. Thin and wonky it was propped up with unstable wooden rods and pegged down with metal skewers. You couldn't sleep in it overnight – it was too cramped to stretch out inside – but a small tribe of Indians could kneel behind the flap and keep a look-out for buffaloes. All my mates came round with their bows and arrows and feathered headdresses to war dance around the tent until their parents sent reinforcements to round them up for tea.

Generally the avenue was the place to play. We lived in a cul-de-sac so few cars ventured up our street and if they did we stared them out until they reluctantly reversed into the main road. Boys played in the road; the pavement, often chalked for hopscotch, was reserved for girls. Or their mums who pushed perambulators around to show off their latest offspring sweltering in knitted bonnets and bootees. Blue for a boy, pink for a girl. We despised the girls who copied them pushing their Pedigree dollies about in toy prams or swanning around in mum's high heels and headscarves pretending to be grown-up.

Every day I played with my friends – Brian Tyer, Peter Dry, Eric Swatton, Derek Harris, Michael Lewis, Richard Turner, Richard Swift, Barry and Kenneth Dutton. Just a few girls were tolerated if they could climb trees or jump streams. We shared scooters, tricycles and brand new bikes which appeared regularly after birthdays or Christmas. We raced on stilts, pogo sticks, roller skates or the go-carts which were then all the rage. We played street soccer under the light of the solitary swan-neck lamp with its fragmented glass shade which served as the single goal post. We argued and squabbled, we fought and fell out . . .

but for more than a decade I grew up in this loyal company which formed The Carter Avenue Gang.

One night there was a terrible tragedy. Great commotion as fire engines with brass bells clanging raced along the avenue. One of the prefabs at the far end of the lane had caught fire! It disappeared in no time – the entire building engulfed in flames. Nothing could be saved and we never heard of the occupants again. 'Those poor people,' Mother moaned into her handkerchief. 'It was a warning to us all.' Next day we hauled our bikes over the wire mesh fence and cycled around the raised foundations of the burnt out prefab. They were still smouldering.

Winter evenings I was content to play alone indoors on the half-moon hearth rug in front of the coal fire. Father studied the daily newspaper (the *Sketch* or *Herald*) while mother unravelled skeins of wool. Favourite toys were plastic cowboys and indians with movable parts and interchangeable features called Swoppits; a toy cannon which fired spent matchsticks and a Hornby speed boat which took a chunk out of the bathroom sink.

One construction set which I hugely enjoyed was Bayko. This 'Master building system for boys and girls' was marketed by Meccano. It comprised a green base with tiny metal rods onto which you slid red or white plastic building blocks plus green doors, windows and a roof. The top set gave you the components to build a lifeboat shelter, sports pavilion or a heliport. My set was grade O, which meant I was limited to a poultry house, seaside shelter or church lychgate. When the box fell apart I stored the kit in a brown leather gas mask case minus its straps.

But best of all – very best of all – was my Hornby Dublo train set. This consisted of an oval circuit of three-rail tracks and a superbly detailed model engine, *The Duchess of Athol*, which either pulled three dark brown carriages or doubled as a goods train. It gave hours of pleasure as it steamed round and round the eternal oval track speeding over the level crossing, flying through the tunnel and occasionally stopping to set down giddy passengers at the solitary, unconvincing, metal station. Slowly, bit by bit, uncles and aunts added

16

buildings to create an entire model village. I still have that trainset, which is stored away within its original pinstriped royal blue box under the stairs – a perfect post-war village in miniature.

Real steam trains ran three times an hour between Deal and London. In addition to the up and the down lines there were two centre tracks carrying goods trains into sidings alongside Deal station. There was a booking office clerk to issue tickets plus several porters to help carry luggage. The stationmaster was a most important official. He wore a clerical grey suit with a waistcoat, in the top pocket of which was a gold watch which he consulted to check the times of departure. At the precise moment he blew his silver whistle and the guard waved his green flag. The locomotive hissed and spat like a scolded cat and reluctantly departed.

Mum and I used to lean over the parapet of an adjacent bridge as the trains passed underneath so we could be engulfed in billowing smoke. At other times we would race to stand underneath a bridge by the park to feel the reverberations as the train rattled and rumbled overhead.

Steam trains are regarded as romantic nowadays but in reality they were a tortuous mode of transport – crowded, dirty, smelly and inordinately slow. Invariably when we visited our relatives in Derby we travelled in the cramped third class carriages with their desultory Southern green livery. On the few occasions when they paid a return visit to our prefab we went to greet them at the station but always misjudged their time of arrival. Auntie Ethel once sent her luggage on ahead but it never arrived so she spent her holiday in borrowed clothes. Grandma, when taken for her first glimpse of the sea in her seventies, cried her eyes out with emotion. 'I never thought there would be so much of it!' she said.

Only occasionally did we have visitors to stay at the prefab. The most feared was Aunt Polly. At the time I had no idea of her exact relationship to our family but upon reflection I think she may have been my great aunt, sister to Pop. Mother dreaded her arrival. You could tell. She swept and dusted twice. One year Aunt Polly wrote ahead to command me to meet her at the coach station

as she had a present for me. A calculated bribe.

This prim, sharp, elderly Welsh matron paraded me in front of her – 'My, how he's grown' – and began to interrogate me as Mother nervously poured tea. There was no mention of a present until at the very last minute she produced a *shirt*. An Hawaiian shirt, she exclaimed, fashionable in America. The Carter Avenue Gang did not follow fashion and I imagined the scorn of all my mates if I dared wear this jazzy garment in the street. Mother admired the pattern as I tried it on and marched with it around the lounge to Aunt Polly's satisfaction. The minute she'd gone Mother pronounced it 'loud', stuffed it in a drawer and took me to Woolworth's to buy me a Dan Dare ray gun.

My own clothes were far from stylish. Jeans and wellingtons were the order of the day, which allowed you to swing from the branches of trees or splash through puddles without appearing unduly scraggy. In summer I was forced to wear a T-shirt and a floppy sunhat so that I resembled Bill or Ben. One winter Gran knitted me a balaclava reminiscent of wartime which I detested as I felt I was being suffocated. I cried and cried until Mother yanked it off.

Smart outdoor wear for children consisted of grey cotton shirt, grey V- neck sweater and grey shorts with button flies and snake clasp belt. Grey, grey, grey . . . Lads did not expect to wear long trousers until the second or third year of secondary school. My long socks kept slipping down so Mother made me elastic garters which bit into my calves. Warm underwear was invariably string vest and pants. A gaberdine mackintosh with a sou'wester or a duffel coat with a hood kept me warm and dry in winter. There was an austere drabness about our world which only broke free in the 1960s with The Beatles.

Dad always relaxed in a hand-knitted cardigan, corduroy trousers with turn-ups and brown suede shoes. On occasions to appear flash he sported an open neck shirt with a cravat and a diamond patterned Fair Isle jersey. Mum went for colour rather than fashion and she was an expert at what she called 'coordinates'. She had a variety of blouses and full skirts pinched at the waist, including one reversible skirt jet black one side, buttercup yellow on the other. Indoors she might wear trousers ('trews') which were practical and comfortable but still considered mannish and rather common as they had been worn in wartime by land girls or workers in munitions factories.

On Saturday night Mum and Dad went dancing. Mum would have all the excitement of selecting an outfit from her limited wardrobe. The pleated skirt, perhaps, or maybe the large polka dots . . ? Her outfit was complete with the new nylon stockings – she never went out without first checking, 'Are my seams straight?' – and black stiletto-heeled shoes. Stilettos always caused a problem. Mother practised walking in them for hours before she could confidently wear them out of doors. Dance floors became so pitted with these sharp heels that rubber tips became compulsory.

Gran came to baby-sit most weekends. I scorched by the fire in my pyjamas reading the latest edition of *Sunny Stories* while she listened intently to the wireless. *Saturday Night Variety Playhouse* presented by Vic Oliver invariably included a fifteen minute drama, starring Jack Hulbert and Cicely Courtneidge, whose plots I vividly recall. Vaudeville acts numbered Alan Melville, Hylda Baker, Elsie and Doris Waters and the delectable Mrs Shufflewick. While we chortled at their tame antics we sipped mugs of Horlicks, Ovaltine, cocoa or Bourne-Vita and crunched Garibaldi, custard creams, arrowroot or ginger nut biscuits.

The radio gave a choice of Home, Light or Third. We preferred the Light station which gave such wonderful programmes early every evening. The entire family listened enthralled by first class entertainment in a room lit only by the light of the dial. An alternative was the fading Radio Luxembourg presenting non-stop pop music by famous rock stars. As teenagers we requested singles by the baby-faced Cliff Richard, the sobbing Johnny Ray or the crooning Frankie Vaughan to be played in sound proof booths at record shops. We had no intention of buying.

Television was a late arrival in our home. The first tv was bought by Mrs Dry at number 10 to entertain her increasingly large family. Probably she acquired her set with its nine inch screen to coincide with the broadcasting of the Queen's Coronation. I bet it set them back a whacking 55 guineas! The entire avenue used to crowd into her cramped sitting room – curtains drawn – to watch after- noon television on special occa- sions. Children's Hour was partic- ularly popular and for the first time our street was deserted an hour before teatime.

Our television was worth wait- ing for – a Decca with slid- ing doors and a seventeen inch

19

screen! When it arrived we made a firm promise we would ration our viewing so that it would not change our lifestyle. But soon we were watching everything screened from *Dotto* to the white dot which appeared at close-down after *The Epilogue*. We regarded the charming announcers, Chris Chataway and Sylvia Peters, as close friends. Father enjoyed the Parisian detective *Maigret*; mother preferred the glamour of *Come Dancing*. Gran allowed me to sit up late viewing in my pyjamas when my parents were out, ready to fly into bed when the garden gate squeaked. There was the whispered promise: 'I'll tell you what happens in the morning'. A few programmes were totally unsuitable for young people. Often a warning was given to alert 'viewers of a nervous disposition'. I remember watching the six episodes of *Quatermass and The Pit* through a crack in the door!

One November evening in 1954 – I would have been six years old – a hurricane brewed up from nowhere. As the rain battered on the windows we listened to the radio in our kitchen to hear dreadful news at sea. The South Goodwin lightship had parted her riding cable and capsized with loss of all hands on the treacherous Goodwin Sands. 'That's near here,' cried Mother, trying hard to conceal her alarm. 'Those poor people.' We sat dismayed as another violent gust of wind threatened to lift the roof off our vulnerable home.

National events – tragedies and triumphs – filtered through to our prefab mainly by the wireless or newspapers, and eventually television. My parents took time to explain important affairs, realising that children are not only curious but naturally resilient. Mount Everest was conquered by Sir Edmund Hillary; Roger Bannister ran the four minute mile; the Munich Airport disaster destroyed the Manchester United Football Team; the Queen opened Gatwick Airport; the Russians launched Laika the dog into space and their Sputnik landed on the Moon; Britain exploded its first H-bomb in the Central Pacific and the Aldermaston marchers protested against research into nuclear weapons.

In the fifties the Festival of Britain promoted Britain's national achievements on London's South Bank where the wafer thin aluminium sculpture, Skylon, mesmerised patrons as it poised in mid air. Princess Margaret ended her romance with Peter Townsend and Prince Charles was created Prince of Wales. Sir Anthony Eden averted the Suez Crisis; Khruschev was elected Prime Minister of Russia and General de Gaulle became Prime Minister of France. The last conscripts for National Service reported for duty. London smog brought devastation to the capital. Volkswagons were the most popular cars. Donald Campbell broke the water speed record in Bluebird on Coniston Water (at 248.62 mph) and the SRN1 Hovercraft made its first direct crossing from Calais to Dover. More importantly for my family food rationing ended, purchase tax was abolished and Premium Bonds were introduced.

Attitudes still reflected the Victorian age. Our country was still nominally Christian. Judges donned a black cap before pronouncing the death sentence; young offenders could be ordered to be birched. Suicide was illegal. Animals did not have rights. Coloured people were regarded as inferior. Seaside landladies often advertised 'No blacks'. Men and women did not receive equal pay. Gentlemen doffed their hats, walked on the outside of the pavement and gave up their seats for ladies. Women never entered a public house unescorted. Men never pushed prams.

There were three distinct divisions of society: upper, middle and working classes. The age of majority was firmly set at 21. Couples did not live openly together. Divorce was rare. Sex hadn't been invented. No-one swore in public. There were frequent end-of-the-world predictions. There was one total eclipse of the sun. Debutantes were presented at court. Bikinis appeared on the beaches. Village bobbies rode bicycles. Women flaunted fur coats. A pint of mild was more popular than bitter. Footballs were brown leather; loo rolls were stark white . . .

Prime Minister Harold Macmillan made his famous pronouncement: 'You've never had it so good'. Our aim in life nonetheless was to continue to better ourselves. Yet Father's low wages as assistant manager at the Co-op (£5 per week when the national average was £9 14s 6d) made it impossible for us to move home because the average price for a three bedroom house was £2,280. Young couples who raised large families or who had children of both sexes were entitled to jump the queue for newly built council houses. We watched with envy as our neighbours the Duttons, the Swifts, the Drys, the Simms, the Bartletts, were successfuly rehoused.

Eventually our chance came. Incredibly, Father had secured a mortgage on an end-of-terrace house near the seafront. It had rooms galore including a dining room, breakfast room, utility rooms, three bedrooms and two attics which I could use as playrooms.

So at the end of the decade we moved into our first proper house. Mum cried when the new occupant arrived prematurely at the prefab to take measurements for curtains. Up until the last moment when the modest removal van came for our sparse furniture we jealously guarded our cosy prefabricated post-war home.

HOME TRUTHS

I CANNOT remember what had upset me, but whatever it was had struck deep . . . so much so that, aged nine or ten, I decided I had no option than to leave home. I went into my bedroom and lifted my small brown leather suitcase from the top shelf of the wardrobe and began to fill it with clothes. Mother came into the room and, noting my distress, offered to help me pack. There was great deliberation, I do recall, as to which tie I should take with me.

Carrying my suitcase, gaberdine mac and pack of banana sandwiches wrapped in greaseproof paper, I made my tearful farewell and walked determinedly away from the prefabs.

There was a plot of scrubland near the school with hides among clumps of bushes which only our gang knew about, so I squatted down to sulk while avoiding the convoy of police cars, tracker dogs and air-sea rescue helicopters which my mother, by now, would have alerted. Left alone with no playmates I tidied off the sticky sandwiches and settled down to doze with only my thoughts for company. The day was long, dark clouds began to form and as the sun started to go down I sensed it was time to return home. I had, after all, made my point and staying out all night had never been my intention.

When I entered by the kitchen door I was surprised to find that it was not yet midday but Mum – bless her – was busy cooking my favourite meal of egg and chips. We ate our lunch in happy silence across the enamel top of the modern mangle which was occasionally converted into a table. Just for two.

Generally, though, my childhood was a time when I felt loved and secure. My parents' wedding photograph stood in an unsteady frame on the dropleaf table in the hall as if to announce to visitors that here lived a Happy Family (the ceremony had taken place in Derby to save Dad's numerous relatives from travelling). Mum stood for the camera in her 1940s wedding dress, with its short train, holding a bouquet of gardenias and beaming radiantly through her flowing veil beside my youthful father, handsomely suited, with his second-thoughts smile.

Now my family extended to the entire avenue. All the neighbours were called Aunt This or Uncle That. Doors were left open or unlocked. We were constantly in and out of each other's houses borrowing foodstuff, offering advice or exchanging gossip, particularly during elevenses. Everyone helped out by looking after children while mothers worked, and babysitters were never a problem. We were not suspicious of strangers. We welcomed them. Guests were the most important members of our household.

The Carter Avenue gang piled into the street at every opportunity for fun and games. There were few cars then so it was safe to do so but also there was a real sense of community in the 1950s. Even amongst kids. A few of the games had been around since time immemorial but they swiftly disappeared when television became mass entertainment at the end of the decade. Grandmother's Footsteps, Piggy in the Middle and What's The Time, Mr Wolf? were great favourites. We also played chain tag and British Bulldog which, through violence, had been banned from the school playground.

Ginger knocking was frowned upon by adults but great fun for kids! We tied string to strangers' knockers (there were no chimes or fancy bells) hid out of sight and pulled it, then ran away laughing when they answered the door to nobody. As a last resort we kicked a tin can around the grass verges or sailed walnut shell boats along rainwater streams in the gutter.

We had a rich street vocabulary with colourful expressions. 'You can't do that for toffee', was one taunt predicting failure while 'She thinks she's the bees knees' dismissed someone who thought themselves too high and mighty. 'Jeepers creepers!', 'What a swizz!', 'I'll have your guts for garters!' One phrase copied from the teddy boys, 'See you later, alligator' was coupled with the rhyming reply, 'In a while, crocodile'.

There were a great number of crazes that swept across the country appealing to both adults and children. Mainly they originated in America. A few of my chums were expert at keeping yo-yos in motion for hours on end but I never got the hang of them. Hula hoops were large plastic circles in bright colours which you twirled round and round your waist. This was considered wonderful exercise so the craze was adopted by mothers for keeping trim. Pogo sticks resembled stilts with springs. You gripped bicycle handles and pushed down hard with both feet simultaneously and if successful hopped along the pavement. Like Skippy the kangaroo.

A few toys were shared, without parents' permission, by the whole street. Tricycles, scooters and pedal cars, which were hard on the knees, were desirable objects. Everyone took turns. Christmases and birthdays heralded brand new bikes which were ridden by their proud owners round and round our cul-de-sac. Homemade stilts were also great fun but best of all were go-carts.

Every boy was a proud owner of a go-cart in the 1950s. First you acquired three stout planks of wood to make the structure. Next you tracked down some discarded pram wheels on rubbish dumps and begged an orange box from the green-grocer's to make a seat. Dads were always willing to construct the body

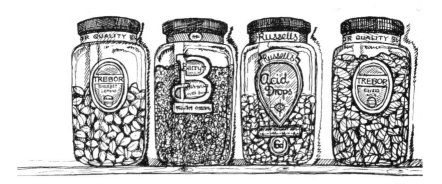

and oil the nuts and bolts for a smooth performance. Refinements might include a cushioned seat and a masthead with a sail to catch the wind.

Once completed, your cart was hauled up an incline and you then persuaded a mate to give you a starter push downhill. Craftily, the mate would hop on the back for a free ride! You steered by means of your feet and a rope attached to the pivotted front wheels. There were no brakes. To stop you simply put your foot down (risky) or skidded into a bank for a crash landing.

There were one or two forbidden toys. Homemade catapults for aiming at wild birds; sheath knives for wittling sharp sticks and peashooters for annoying rival gangs by trying to ping their ears. Older brothers brandished flick knives until they were declared illegal.

Girls played separately. We tended to ignore them as they trundled baby brothers or sisters in pushchairs along the pavement or flounced around in their nurses' uniforms (popularised by ITV's *Emergency Ward 10*) While we fought at cops and robbers or cowboys and indians they made daisy chains or cats' cradles. Sometimes we allowed them to hold buttercups under our chins to tell by the reflection if we liked butter. Generally girls appeared far too grown up, clipclopping in their mums' high heels, wearing smears of make up and plastic jewellery (free with *Girl* or *Bunty*). We taunted shy girls with pink National Health spectacles, or braces on their front teeth, and pulled their plaits and pony tails. There was a sense of triumph when we sent them crying to their mothers.

The one place where boys and girls met was at children's parties. At intervals Mother would drag me along to one of the neighbours' prefabs. She would push me into the centre of the room where I stood conspicuously – Brylcreamed hair and centre parting, squeaky shoes and wrapped gift – instantly shy and tongue tied in company. Cheerful mums would pair us off to play parlour games – Oranges and Lemons, Farmer's in his Den, Pass The Parcel, Pin the Tail on the Donkey – before being ushered into tea.

26

Butter wouldn't melt in my mouth as I took my place at table. I had been primed to eat a fair share of bread and butter before jelly and cake. Teatime rules, apparently, did not apply to the village kids who spurned the savouries and attacked the sweets with gusto. There were soft rolls we called huffkins, sausage rolls, cheese straws and blancmange. Flavoured jellies were served in frilly waxed paper cups, accompanied by cylinders of Walls ice cream. Finally, lights dimmed for the presentation birthday cake – rich fruit topped with marzipan and icing, decorated with plastic figures and the appropriate number of candles to be blown out with one PUFF! Before I left I was mindful to recite my rehearsed speech: 'Thank you for having me'. Next day, truce over, the boys would be back playing sword fights while the girls nursed their dollies.

Sweets were sold in jars and bought loose by the quarter pound. They were scooped out, weighed precisely on brass scales and wrapped in paper bags. Here is a selection: liquorice comfits, cough candy, sherbet pips, mixed berries, winter mixture, aniseed twists, pineapple cubes, coconut mushrooms, acid drops, mint imperials, pink and white iced caramels and pear drops which smelt like nail varnish. There were also sherbet dabs and jamboree bags which held a selection of sweets plus a mystery gift. Liquorice allsorts, sugar mice, jelly babies and dolly mixture remain popular today. Oddities were flying saucers that contained sherbet, jelly watches you could wear on your wrist and penny whistles which you could eat after blowing!

Wrapped bars of chocolate were regarded as a luxury. Maltesers, Milky Way, Kit Kat and Crunchie bars are still around today. Fry's sold the most popular bars. Their Five Boys chocolate wrapper featured five identical boys whose expressions changed from misery to joy as you munched your way through the chocolate. There were tubes of Smarties, Refreshers and Polo Mints. Palm toffee bars had sickly fillings such as Banana Split, Liquorice Nougat and Treacle Sandwich. For adults there were presentation boxes of Milk Tray,

Weekend and Black Magic contained in a striking black and silver Art Deco package.

Occasionally Mum treated me to a Snowball (marshmallow covered in coconut flakes) or a Wagon Wheel (an enormous round biscuit coated in chocolate). Spangles were enjoyed by the whole family, particularly the liquorice flavour, which when introduced was a real surprise. Bubble gum was discouraged by parents but popular with kids. You could blow it into a gigantic bubble until it smacked against your lips!

Best of all were the selections of confectionery laid out in trays at the front of a sweet shop counter. You could keep customers waiting a long time while you made your choice and felt grand when you handed over one penny for four items. There were black jacks, milk chews, sugar shrimps and liquorice bootlaces. Large gobstobbers cost a whole penny. They filled your entire mouth in one go and had the extra attraction of changing colour as you sucked them.

Gran attempted to introduce healthy eating and for a time her delicacies held a certain novelty. Pomegranates were sliced in half and eaten with the aid of a pin to pick out pips surrounded by pink pulp. Liquorice twigs had a revolting taste but it was great fun gnawing at those woody sticks. Best treat of all though was a whole honeycomb!

There were a number of children's diseases to be feared in postwar Britain. German measles, mumps and chicken pox did the rounds and mothers in their wisdom made sure their children played with an infected child so that they could get these ailments over with early in life. Tuberculosis, diphtheria and whooping cough were dreaded because they were often fatal. Hot summers produced an epidemic of poliomyelitis which crippled and killed hundreds of children in the fifties. At school we were vaccinated against most diseases but the inoculation for polio took the form of swallowing a doctored sugar lump which was fairly palatable.

Occasionally I was whisked off to hospital, for the removal of adenoids and tonsils, although I managed to retain my appendix (quite a feat for the time). Matrons were brusque and nurses unsympathetic to the plight of sickly children. When I fell down the chalk face of a building site it was almost with apology that my parents sought medical help. Father held me down screaming as the nurse bathed the terrific gash in my leg and the surgeon stitched up the wound – all without anaesthetic.

Almost as much feared as the hospital was the monthly haircut. Again without anaesthetic. Mum would collect me from school and escort me to the barber's at Upper Deal. When I was very young she used to sit with me alongside all the men who were suddenly on their best behaviour. When I grew older she

28

tended to pay the barber in advance and leave me alone to wait – a shy figure hidden among the hats and coats.

A wooden bench was fixed to the walls and you slid along, one at a time, until it was your turn to be shorn. There was a pile of musty newspapers and magazines for you to peruse as you waited for what seemed ages. The newest stack was *Picture Post* with its dramatic news photographs. Sometimes the men would allow me to jump the queue – was this through kindness or to escape their embarrassment when asking the barber for 'something for the weekend?' (On whispered cue he would reach surreptitiously inside a wall cabinet stocked with Rizzla cigarette papers and Gillette razor blades for what looked like a packet of three very plain party balloons).

The barber in his stained white coat placed a padded wooden plank across the arms of the stout tilting wooden chair for me to sit level with the sink facing the mirror. He swished a gigantic white cape over me so that my head stuck out like a plum pudding on a tablecloth. Mindful to ask on which side I had my parting, he located my crown and then attacked my mousey locks with electric clippers. Short back and sides was the order of the day. Mum could not abide the trend for American crew cuts. Any way there was a firm notice: 'No trims, no styles'.

The barber tucked a strip of cotton wool inside my shirt collar to stop itchy hairs slipping down my back. I shuddered when the cold steel of the clippers touched my nape and sneezed when he blew talc from a red rubber puffer to soothe the abrasion. Deftly he would unhook a hand mirror from the wall and hold it behind my head waiting for my nod of approval. As a final touch he either sprayed Brilliantine to calm my stinging scalp or alternatively he rubbed Brylcream into my hair so that it shone with health. A proper gentleman.

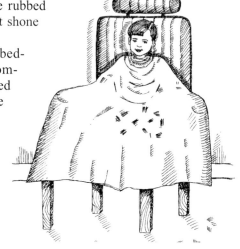

Once while rummaging in a bedroom drawer I discovered a complete barber's set which belonged to my grandfather. Presumably he had ambitions of earning a living as a travelling hairdresser in the period of depression before the war. In the zip-up leather case there was a chrome pot containing cotton wool, several bottles of after-shave, a neck brush, a tor-

29

toisehell comb and chunky scissors. Plus a pair of clippers that cried out for experimentation.

Derek Harris arrived at the very moment of discovery and succumbed to my enthusiastic imitations of the fashionable London hairdresser, Teezie Weezie. I lopped and cropped and snipped and shaped. Hair fell in handfulls with each tug of the clippers. I was in full stride when my mother called me in for lunch. A few mouthfuls later there was furious knocking at the kitchen door. Mrs Harris burst in with her offspring and tearfully complained I had ruined her son's hair. This seemed unreasonable since I had only shorn him down one side and anyway the result on top was quite artistic. All the same it was my turn to receive a clip round the ear.

Mother was always smartly dressed. Although she had a limited wardrobe she was skilful at that style known as 'mix and match' – combining colourful scarves, blouses, cardigans and skirts – so that you could never recall her wearing the same outfit twice. On formal occasions she would sport a clutch bag, long gloves and a dainty hat with a plume or veil worn at a rakish angle.

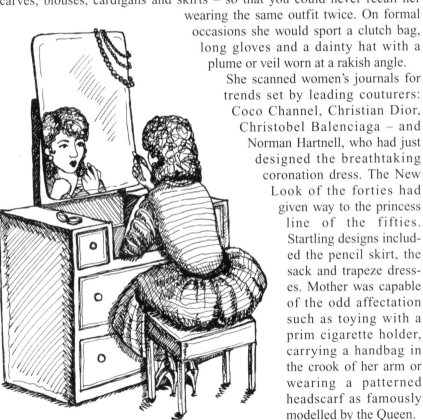

She scanned women's journals for trends set by leading couturiers: Coco Channel, Christian Dior, Christobel Balenciaga – and Norman Hartnell, who had just designed the breathtaking coronation dress. The New Look of the forties had given way to the princess line of the fifties. Startling designs included the pencil skirt, the sack and trapeze dresses. Mother was capable of the odd affectation such as toying with a prim cigarette holder, carrying a handbag in the crook of her arm or wearing a patterned headscarf as famously modelled by the Queen.

On occasions when Mum was getting all dolled up for a party I watched mesmerised as she applied her make-up in the mirror. First she smoothed Max Factor pancake over her face using a damp sponge. Next she painted a true red bow with her Tangee lipstick, blotted her lips with a tissue and carefully added a second coat. Eyebrows she attacked with a pencil before brushing her eyelashes with mascara to accentuate their length. When she felt daring she might be tempted to add a beauty spot. Lastly, she dabbed perfume behind her ears – Bourjois' Evening in Paris. Mum was mindful to slip her powder compact and mirror into her handbag so that she could retouch her make-up during the course of the evening.

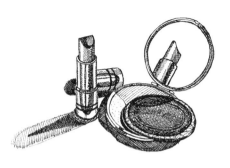

The dressing table would then be scattered with the contents from her vanity case: Pond's Cold Cream, Coty face powder, Nivea hand cream, Yardley Old English Lavender talc . . . In addition there would be a manicure set, nail varnish, scent sprays and hair curlers which she slept in overnight and removed first thing in the morning.

While she dressed there might be a brief glimpse of her underwear as she attached her nylons to her suspenders before pulling down her petticoat. Once I watched with amusement as she practised walking up and down our lounge in a dead straight line in her peep-toe high heels, holding her 'cheeks' tight so that her short skirt flounced provocatively in imitation of Marilyn Monroe. The American film star's celebrated wiggle, we learned later, was contrived by having one heel shorter than the other!

Mum had a little jewellery which she kept in a case on her dressing table. When she lifted the lid a plastic ballerina pirouetted to tinkly music and her jerky gyrations were reflected in an oval mirror. Her favourite piece was a string of Poppets – beads which locked together to form a long chain. Apart from her wedding ring there was not a trace of gold nor silver. Costume jewellery consisted of diamanté, paste or mother-of-pearl. Valuable pieces were likely to be marcasite – earrings, bracelets and a cocktail watch worn over a long white glove – which added distinctive glitter to her evening outfits.

There was one delightful brooch – an embroidered pair of bluebirds in an oval frame worn at the neck in the centre of a blouse. Mum may have worked this herself because embroidery was still an essential craft engaged in by young mothers. She painstakingly embroidered handkerchiefs, tray cloths,

31

runners and a set of cushions. She would first iron a transfer onto a plain white cloth and then delicately sew silks in a charming pattern. I loved the vibrant shades of the silks and admired the results of her handiwork. Invariably the design was of a crinoline lady with a parasol and poke bonnet against a background of foxgloves and hollyhocks in a country garden.

Ideas, and free transfers, often came from her three weekly magazines, *Woman, Woman's Own* and *Woman's Realm*. The glossy pages gushed ideas for self and home improvements. Recipes, baby wear, knitting patterns, handy hints. The note was one of practicality and reinforced the idea that a woman's place was in the home. Monica Dickens analysed experiences of life; Eileen Fowler demonstrated keep fit; Constance Spry suggested flower arrangements; Beverley Nichols trilled about his cats. There were romantic stories (without a hint of sex) and problem pages with readers' letters headed: *He wants me to wait, She's a spendthrift,* and *His friend comes too.* For children there were comic strips featuring Richmal Crompton's lovable rascal William, and a twee series about a family of robins. Mother learned how to knit her own briefs and bra, make marrow chutney, embroider a cottage tea cosy, sew rabbit skin gloves . . .

The Make Do and Mend of the wartime years gave way to Do It Yourself during the late 1950s. People felt compelled to make needless home improvements inspired by Barry Bucknell whose television programme on household hints was essential viewing for the middle and lower classes. The 'nook and cranny' period homes were revamped by amateurs who covered up panelled doors, fireplaces and bannisters with hardboard and Formica.

Advertisements in magazines and, later, television targeted young married couples and tended to make them dissatisfied with their humble postwar homes. Illustrations of ideal homes constantly paraded the attainable before newlywed homemakers but modern manufacturers of furniture and furnishings rarely made an impact on our fifties prefab. We admired studio couches which converted into spare beds, telephone tables incorporating padded seats, trios of occasional tables which neatly stacked away and magazine racks with raffia sides and cocktail cherry feet. A picture of a Chinese girl whose luminous green complexion resembled a housefly was inexplicably popular in millions of modern homes.

Lights were particularly imaginative: garish television lamps had knobbly plastic shades and sputnik legs; ceiling rocket lights cascaded over the sitting room while rise and fall lights brought atmosphere above the dining table. Marley thermoplastic tiles brightened kitchen floors although posh homes might afford expensive wooden parquet blocks. Fabrics tended to reflect the room, thus seagulls and seashells were for bathrooms; plates and fruit were for kitchens.

Woolworth's Homemaker range of china with its silhouette design of household furniture was collected, and Melamine dinner services were equally popular since they were practically unbreakable. The one thing my mother longed for was a Goblin Cheerywake Teasmade combining bedside lamp, alarm clock and tea maker won by contestants on television game shows.

The idea of keeping up with the Joneses had a poignancy in our home since mother's maiden name *was* Jones. At first my parents struggled to pay professionals, which at times had disastrous results. The decorators once hung floral wallpaper upside down (but we grew to like it). They returned while I was still a nipper to paper the lounge in fashionable Regency red-and-white stripes. Mother, satisfied by their expertise, dozed in the deep armchair while I took the opportunity for my own attempt at home improvement by sticking gummed shapes around the fireplace. Mother's look of horror when she awoke dispelled any further artistic ambitions. She said nothing but recalled the decorators who worked swiftly to repair the damage before father returned.

The truth was that in a prefab where we had all mod cons there were mighty few improvements

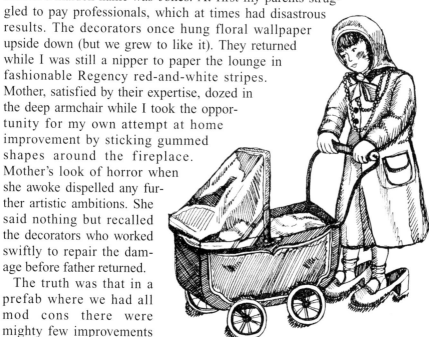

to be made. Lack of space curtailed any ambitious programme of alteration or extension. Council workmen came round every three years to daub dark green paint on the exterior. Interior decoration might, however, be attempted. This was a team effort laboriously scraping the old paper off the walls, mixing the paste and hanging the paper which took ages to dry and was often lumpy. Rolls of paper came with edges which had to be trimmed and because mother often miscalculated the number required we invariably had to order an extra roll whose colour never quite matched. Later improvements in DIY included prepasted wallpaper, paint rollers and power tools first demonstrated at the annual Ideal Home exhibitions at London's Olympia.

Meticulous as always, Dad spent an age in touching up the paintwork on doors, windows, skirting boards and picture rails, selecting pastel shades from the Dulux range. He avoided the vibrant colours (veridian, juniper, zephyr) and plumped for the softer tones (barley, magnolia and duck egg blue). Perhaps people were embarrassed or ashamed of their efforts, for any attempt at decoration was preceded by blanking out the windows with Windoline so that no-one could peer in.

Flock wallpaper became fashionable in the 1950s. My parents declined to hang it, probably because it was expensive, although they told me it would give me asthma. Once I admired a design of cocktail glasses and shakers in vivid grey and scarlet flock. My home of the future, I promised myself, would be covered entirely in this striking design. Dad complained that the one thing our home lacked was a cocktail cabinet. He coveted one shaped like the prow of a sailing ship displayed in the window of Courts. He visualised it with all its accoutrements – chrome cocktail shaker, glass soda siphons, tiger skin ice bucket, glass stirrers in the shape of girlie pin-ups . . . The cabinet never materialised and to be sure it would have been an anachronism since my father was rarely known to stand anyone a drink.

To be fair, Dad, although an amateur, was quite a handyman. He made shelves for the bedroom and pelmets for the lounge. He stuck asbestos tiles to the kitchen ceiling and cut and laid linoleum in the bathroom. Any home improvement was an excuse for a party and a new low coffee table (knees scrunched up tight as you sipped from miniature cups) would be a chance to have the neighbours round to admire your handiwork.

Coffee tables were a decidedly new feature and reflected the trend for hospitality in the home. The rule seemed to be that coffee was drunk in the morning, tea in the afternoon. Tables were often kidney-shaped but occasionally also in the style of an artist's palette. More formal versions might have ceramic tiles on top with a pattern of poodles, ballerinas or a Parisian scene. China coffee sets might be black on the outside with different pastel shades – primrose, turquoise, rose, cream, tangerine, aquamarine – on the inside. A whole series of coffee table books began to appear, concentrating on atmospheric photographs rather than text, and intended for casual browsing while people made polite conversation.

Our prefab never quite achieved the true contemporary look of the 1950s. My parents aimed for space, light and colour in contrast to the depressing chocolate brown, bottle green and nicotine cream of the pre-war years. Their colour scheme was muted compared to what was currently in vogue but at least they achieved a style that was both tasteful and homely.

Only once did I glimpse a luxurious modern open plan apartment boasting mezzanine floor, a mural of a jungle waterfall, room dividers stacked with house plants, sunburst wall clock, an aquarium, television lamps, basket chairs, boomerang coffee tables, fitted carpets, molecular patterned curtains and a breakfast bar copied from the American sit-coms of ITV.

However grand our prefab, most of my life was spent out on the street. We were termed latchkey kids because the front door key was strung round our necks for us to let ourselves in when both our parents were out at work. This did not mean we were not cared for – we were always made welcome in our neighbours' homes – it simply meant we had a vast amount of freedom.

Mums and dads would join in our games by batting at cricket and fielding for rounders. We dodged in and out of pedestrians on our roller skates and watched with disgust as the girls tucked their skirts into their knickers to do handstands. Complete strangers would put down their shopping bags and play hopscotch chalked on the pavement or hitch up their skirts and take a turn at skipping with a borrowed clothes line. 'Keep the kettle boiling, if you miss a loop you're OUT!'

Friday night was bath night. Worse luck! Parents rounded up their offspring skulking in dark corners of the avenue. Father tried hard to dissuade us from bathing more than once a week since it did untold harm, he said, 'opening the pores'. We knew, of course, that this was merely his obsession with the expense of the immersion heater. After Christmas there was the added luxury of bath cubes to dissolve in the water but, failing that, a splash of Dettol made a bath special. The village children envied us this weekly soak because most rural families still shared the contents of a galvanised metal tub in their back yard.

SWINGS AND ROUNDABOUTS

E ARLY one morning – very early – my father woke me and told me to dress in warm clothes while he retrieved our bikes from the shed. We cycled in the morning mist through Mongeham village to fields behind the parish church where we began to hunt for mushrooms.

Fairy rings had appeared magically overnight in the damp velvet grass. In the distance a fox shied, decided we were no threat and slunk away into the hedgerow. Birds interrupted their dawn chorus startled that they had been beaten to their own fields. Sleepily, I held the trug while father located and picked handfulls of large, flat, round mushrooms. At home mother tossed them into a pan of sizzling butter and accompanied with mountains of toast we tucked into a delicious breakfast.

Gran could remember when the prefab and council house estates at Upper Deal were open fields even though she had not long been resident in East Kent. In fact the council houses at Mongeham appeared in my lifetime and before they were built I flew homemade paper kites in the open meadows strewn with buttercups and daisies. From a high bank there was an uninterrupted view over the countryside reaching as far as Dover, where a tall television mast was being rapidly erected on the clifftop.

A rugged path through a paddock was regarded as a short cut to the village where, proud on a hill, stood the dumpy tower of the Norman church. In late summer labourers gathered corn into stooks while we strayed into their farmyard to tumble down hayricks. We threw barley 'darts' and smoked acorn 'pipes'. As we tramped across the footpaths through the prickly stubble we paused to listen to the chirrup of the skylark and strained to spot him miles high in the mackerel sky. With the march of time combine harvesters were introduced and from a safe distance we watched their progress, resentful of this intrusion.

Country lanes reaped further wild harvests. We took baskets to gather black-berries from the hedgerows and were always surprised to meet next-door neighbours with the same idea. Scrumping, however, was regarded more as a game for there was sweet temptation in stealing forbidden fruit. There were several orchards on the outskirts of the village and apples always tasted better after we had evaded the farmer's chase.

One event sticks in my mind. We climbed a low fence to snatch windfalls from a private garden. Although the tree was bare, ripe fruit lay in abundance over the lawn. Apparently, the woman who lodged in the house had learned she was about to be evicted and rather than allow the new tenants to enjoy her labours she violently shook the tree so that the apples fell and rotted on the ground.

Mongeham was a good half a mile from our prefab estate. We were sent on occasional errands, with the coins safely tucked into our mittens, to the village for a forgotten pint of milk from the dairy. But more usually our purpose was one of exploration. We freewheeled our bikes down a hill, cycled straight past the chapel, two inns and a garage and then sped round a curve by the parish hall. We pushed our bikes uphill as far as St Martin's Church, twisted and turned down Cherry Lane – festooned with blossom in spring – and came to a halt by the Post Office. The scene was full of contrast; grand houses mingled with farmyards, a filling station sidled with thatched cottages.

In the crescent-shaped field by the parish hall cubs might be pitching their tents for a jamboree, or teenagers from the chapel holding their 'sausage siz-zle' (a grand name for a barbecue). Youngsters could be making a scarecrow in their banked allotment or a gardener with a battered hat and a pipe would be transporting his prize marrow in a wobbly wheelbarrow to the annual horti-cultural show. One afternoon I was startled to see a woman in a sunhat at the top of a ladder picking mulberries from a shored tree. The lush scarlet berries were staining her white overall. From a distance it looked like dripping blood.

At times a marquee was pitched in the bottom field to hold a flower show and a gymkhana might be in progress in the top meadow opposite the church. At such events Prefab Kids were regarded as outsiders and were not made to feel welcome.

We could, of course, hold our own flower festival (my ideas were generally acted upon by the gang). Purposely, I pitched my wigwam in the back garden. Inside I laid planks across bricks to make platforms around the perimeter. Secretly, I sent scouts in search of specimens for our display. Adults eagerly queued up that afternoon and paid the ha'penny admission fee to view the

Carter Avenue Horticultural Show. I could never understand the parents' dismay at seeing their prize blooms now stuck in jam jars and wilting in the cramped interior of the tent. Yet another clip round the ear seemed a poor reward for introducing culture to the neighbourhood!

Trenches were cut in the scrubland behind our prefabs. They zigzagged for miles. Presumably they had have been dug by troops practising manoeuvres during the recent war. We crawled on our bellies through the shallow tunnels and fired at each other with sticks wittled at one end to resemble rifles. Real squabbles took place only when mates refused to play 'dead'.

Making camps was an important part of our childhood. We built several 'hides' with vantage points in the wasteland behind our prefabs. We collected planks of wood, cardboard boxes and scraps of corrugated iron to make a tent where we would meet in secret, Blyton style, after whispering a pre-arranged password. There was great dismay on occasions when we discovered that rival gangs had invaded our territory and rummaged through our private property.

A most secret place was The Rookery. Tall trees grew on either side of a narrow dirt track leading to open fields. High, overhead, rooks rode in their nests swaying alarmingly like ships tossed on a stormy sea. Soil had

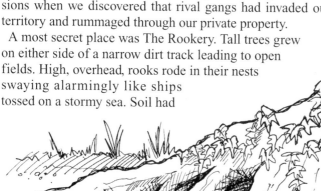

eroded from the banks so that the roots were exposed to resemble witches' fingers. You could pass unnoticed through a spindly passage from under one tree to another and spy on unsuspecting travellers. A scene of mystery and imagination.

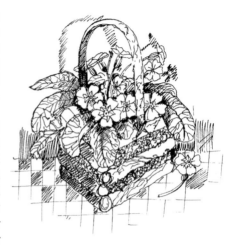

Everyone knew Willow Woods and it was a race to get there in the spring. We cycled out to collect sticky buds, catkins, primroses and bluebells. These we distributed among the neighbours, particularly those who Mum said were ill or elderly and need cheering up. Our wicker cycle baskets would be full of flowers and at home we soon ran out of vases to contain them. All the same we were mindful to leave some for other people to enjoy and refrained from digging roots up although at that time there were no protected species.

Fishing was a social activity for village children. The brooks promised sticklebacks; the marshes yielded minnows. We made fishing rods and nets from gardening sticks, bent nails and muslin strips and tied string round jam jars to hold our catch. There were several streams to cross. You either felled a log to form a bridge or swung from a rope tied to a branch from an adjacent tree. Neither methods of fording were infallible and we usually spent an hour or two drying off clothes on the banks before daring to return home for tea.

Birds nesting was another popular pastime. We climbed the highest trees in pursuit of our prize. The rule was to leave at least one egg for the mother who would otherwise fly away. The whereabouts of the nests of unusual birds such as jays or magpies were considered secrets worth trading. Stolen eggs were blown and displayed along with other treasures such as feathers, shells, bones, fossils or abandoned nests on bedroom shelves. Pocket-size encyclopaedias called Observer books were consulted to identify our speckled trophies. News went round that one of the older lads who lived near the school had captured an eel and we were invited at any time to go and look at it. None of the gang knew what an eel

looked like and our imaginations worked overtime. Perhaps it charged like an elephant; maybe it swooped like a vulture? When we plucked up courage to investigate we were dismayed to find an insignificant slimy shape slithering in a stone sink. Bitterly disappointed we threw stones into the water

hoping to sink the creature and stormed off in disgust in search of a more stimulating pastime.

Snail racing, though slow, passed several happy hours. The hunt was on for the most distinctive gastropod with the biggest shell (although this, of course, did not guarantee speed) We painted numbers on their shells or identified them with sticky shapes and sent them sprinting down the straight on the racecourse chalked on the pavement. They did not all start at once nor did they always run in the required direction but an occasional prod with a twig was all they needed to spur them on to victory. Winners were highly prized and awarded a life of luxury in a laurel leaf-lined cardboard box.

Wildlife was taken for granted. Nothing was protected or conserved. Our parents had, after all, themselves just survived a world war. Squirrels, hedgehogs, hares, voles were dismissed as uninteresting. A fox, though, was worth more than a passing glance since it displayed individual character. A cub, trapped on a railway line, was rescued by my music teacher and children were allowed to visit the injured animal before it was released into the wild.

Few vehicles drove down our avenue. The usual modes of transport were bicycles, mopeds and motorcycles. Scooters and Lambrettas appeared towards the end of the decade along with Mods and Rockers. Mum and Dad still owned a tandem on which they had leisurely cycled along country lanes in their courting days. Eventually steamrollers appeared to flatten the newly laid tarmac in preparation for the arrival of motor vehicles in

41

Carter Avenue. At first these were delivery vans and the short lived mobile shops which mother declared far too expensive.

Traffic was sparse even in the town centre. There were no parking meters, seat belts, MOTs, breathalyser tests or speed restrictions apart from in urban areas (30 mph), although a doctor suspecting a motorist was driving under the influence of alcohol would demand that he recite tongue twisters and walk a straight line. Kerbstones in some towns were still painted black and white as a wartime precaution and policemen in white gloves directed traffic at cross-roads before the installation of traffic lights.

Our friendly neighbour, George Gibb, a miner, acquired one of the first cars in Carter Avenue – a Ford Prefect. He bought the car on the strength of my father's promise that he would teach him to drive in return for sacks of coal. Dad had gained his licence during the war when he drove lorries pulling gun carriages with ammunition trailers, as well as chauffering the Colonel in Burma.

Mr Gibb's car was a black, four door, family saloon with an 8hp engine and a starter motor. Orange semaphore indicators flicked out to show whether he intended turning left or right. Prior to his driving test he practised hand signals by sitting on a kitchen chair and waving his arm in frantic gestures while father prompted from a Highway Code. Turning left (arm rotating anti-clock-wise) turning right (arm straight out) or moving straight ahead (hand raised).

On cold frosty mornings he struggled to crank up the engine and disappeared

underneath the bonnet, cursing, in his greasy overalls, on dark winter evenings. 'Uncle' George's Ford Prefect seemed permanently parked on the pavement. Even so he was the envy of the neighbours when he buffed up its bodywork on Sunday mornings.

Ironically my father couldn't afford his own car until the early 1960s. It was worth waiting for, an Austin 1100, stylish, comfy and shaded such a dark green it appeared almost black.

Shortly afterwards he courageously drove the family on the newly opened motorways to see his relatives in Derby. A pile of sixpenny *News Chronicle* I Spy books kept me quiet in the back seat for this interminable journey. Their subjects ranged from *On the Road* to *In Hospital, On The Farm* to *At The Zoo*. By completing them I hoped to win further colour coded feathers (seashore hunter – turquoise; railway traveller – lime green; dog detective – lemon; amateur archaelogist – bright blue) for my Big Chief headdress.

Whenever cars braved our avenue Tex could be relied upon to chase them off. Tex was a black and white terrier – a patch over one eye – who belonged to the street. At nights he went home to the Browns, or was it the Drys? But in the daytime he joined in all our adventures. All the same he refused to accept progress and saw his mission in life to challenge vehicles by attacking their tyres while in motion. What became of him we could only guess but sadly he never attuned to the age of the motor car.

Everyone owned a pet. Cats and dogs were commonplace. They served a practical purpose. Mrs Dutton lent out her cat for a few nights whenever neighbours suspected mice in their prefabs. Puppies and kittens were constantly offered for sale. There were also rabbits, guinea pigs, hamsters and mice. Goldfish won at the fair were squashed into round bowls. Terrapins

fared better in a rectangular aquarium. As a kid I spent hours with my nose pressed up against the pet shop window. My mother reluctantly said I could keep goldfish and I remember requesting the shopkeeper to find one boy and one girl so they could breed. I was an only child and desperately wanted a dog. Father said he couldn't afford the licence (7/6d, which was far more expensive than a marriage licence), but the truth was our prefab was too small for a dog.

Tortoises were popular. Owners painted their names and addresses on their varnished shells. For extra security they drilled holes into the shells by which to attach a string tied to a stake. Often, though, they escaped and burrowed into next door's garden and had to be retrieved.

I had to be different. After visiting a caged bird show in the town I wanted my own collection of exotic birds. Luckily, a breeder was splitting up an aviary and selling birds individually to the local pet shop. I soon had a large collection of love birds and zebra finches, all housed in friends' redundant budgie cages and stacked on the kitchen table.

My great favourite was Rusty. He was a cutthroat, which meant that he looked exactly like a sparrow with a bright red slash across his throat. He was a true friend. Whenever I practised the piano he would puff himself up to twice his size and warble until I stopped. We were rivals in horrendous sounds. Rusty was so tame he could be trusted to be let out each time I cleaned his cage. Whenever he tired of flying around the kitchen he returned to his little home. That, alas, was his downfall. One afternoon when I was at school Gran released him while leaving the window open and my little companion was never seen again.

When I was a youngster I owned a cat. After infant school mother took me to a country house so that I might have my choice of kitten. The liveliest was a ginger tom which we carried home in a wicker shopping basket. His head popped up queriously at moments from under a blanket. It must have been around Christmas because before we got home it had begun to snow.

At first no name sprang to mind as we declined the obvious feline appellations of Ginger, Tommy, Brandy, etc. In the 1950s the entire nation was health conscious, particularly towards young children. Fortunately Mum declined the ghastly free concentrated orange juice offered by the National Health Service (which was later proved to produce aggressive behaviour in American youngsters) but she did force me to take a daily spoonful of cod liver oil and malt as a protection against colds. It tasted repulsive. One day the cat jumped onto the table and helped himself to the sickly concoction. From that moment onwards he was called Malty.

Truth to tell, Malty never really settled with a boisterous toddler in a tiny prefab. Perhaps he secretly resented being the target of a popgun or being dressed up to perform in circuses. When he wandered off for an entire fortnight mother eventually tracked him down living with a couple of elderly spinsters at Mongeham. They were dismayed when he was reclaimed and so, apparently, was the cat. Not long afterwards he disappeared once more and this time completely without trace. Years later mother confessed to me she had again found Malty at the spinsters' cottage but hadn't the heart to wake him from his slumber on the hearthrug in front of their blazing coal fire.

There were picnics – planned or impromptu – when my gang cycled out into the countryside in convoys. Our wicker baskets were crammed with appetising sandwiches – choices of filling included chocolate, biscuits, crisps, sprinkled sugar, Peanut Butter, fish paste, lemon curd or Marmite – and home made pop consisting of liquorice, sherbet or lemonade crystals shaken into a bottle of tap water. When we felt flush we might treat ourselves to a bottle of fizzy Bing, Tizer or Vimto, frothy American cream soda or murky Dandelion and Burdoch. A mate might share a packet of Smith's crisps or some tiger nuts. We might be out all day and no-one bothered. A note on the kitchen table was all that was required to allay our parents' fears for our safety.

Once a year the gypsies came pushing their battered prams in which were stuffed bunches of lifeless flowers. The women wore headscarves and earrings and extraordinary drapes. As soon as you opened the door to them they'd ask: 'Have you

got an old coat you don't want, dearie?', their sharp eyes having instantly seized upon that very same garment hanging in the hall. We chased them off and threw stones at them and called them Gyppos. At the same time we coveted their wares. They sold wooden clothes pegs, twigs with bits of coloured wax attached in the semblance of flowers, and tiny woven baskets in which were planted primroses stolen from Willow Wood.

Occasionally the rag-and-bone man appeared in his van. He would announce his arrival by ringing his handbell and shouting his requirements. We took out bundles of moth-eaten clothes and soiled woollen blankets which his mittened hands eagerly seized to weigh on his portable scales. In fair exchange we were offered plastic windmills on sticks or yet more goldfish in polythene bags.

More regularly, especially in the immediate postwar period, travelling salesmen would knock at the back door tempting us to buy household goods – dusters, brushes, brooms. Invariably they were ex-soldiers, still smartly dressed in their demob suits, who had not yet infiltrated into mainstream society. On principle mother would buy something which she could ill afford because these brush salesmen, she considered, were deserving causes.

Bob-A-Job week brought an army of cubs and scouts all in their smart uniforms who offered to do some work – any work – in return for a shilling (a bob). They hoped, of course, simply for a donation, but they were often called into our house to clean windows, polish silver or merely wash up.

Whenever my mother took me shopping in the town there would be groups of American GIs hanging around the street corners. They were based at nearby Manston Aerodrome, and were the remnants of squadrons retained during the Cold War. Now that the real war was over, much of their glamour was tarnished and they seemed an anachronism ('Over paid, over sexed and over here'). Girls were still attracted to them, however, but my mother was scornful. Their main faults were twofold: they drank straight from bottles and they smoked in the street.

Most people smoked – parents and older brothers and sisters. Pipe racks were features of prefab mantlepieces. Cigarette cases, lighters and ashtrays – some on wooden stands – were prominent. Advertisements glamourising smoking appeared on television and leading brand names were displayed on hoardings. 'Cool as a mountain stream' (Consulate); 'You're never alone with a Strand' (Strand). Children imitated grown ups by buying chocolate cigarettes, liquorice pipes and chewy tobacco.

Great entertainment for our gang was provided free by playing on the building site which had opened up at the back of Carter Avenue. Parents did not consider the possibility of danger befalling their offspring on this unconventional playground. On the contrary mother rehearsed me with a false name and address in case I was arrested by a bobby on his bicycle. My gang romped around each evening at dusk swinging from the scaffolding and flying round the foundations of the new block of flats. For fun we pelted the night watch-

man's hut with stones but nothing would induce him to come out and chase us! The builders had the last laugh all the same for when the road was laid it clearly linked with Carter Avenue. Demolition of our prefabs was imminent.

Quite by chance one evening I strayed into Mongeham and made a thrilling discovery. There, in a field little bigger than a pocket handkerchief, stood a travelling fair. Although it boasted only two or three attractions it still held tremendous magic and enchantment.

There was a try-your-strength machine where stocky farmhands demonstrated their prowess by striking a base with an enormous mallet. An indicator raced to the top of the post where it might ring a bell thus proclaiming to all observers that here was a man with virility and power. A draughty marquee served as a makeshift amusement arcade sporting penny-in-the-slot machines and vertical bagatelles. Tempted gamblers hoped to win their money back plus a trifling sum.

Across one corner stood a red and white striped coconut shy. Village lads rolled up their sleeves and shied wooden balls at bearded coconuts propped defiantly onto hooped wires stuck fast into the ground. Triumphant winners presented their cracked trophies to their sweethearts as a token of their affection. The colourful row of swingboats required strength rather than skill to tug the knotted rope and set up a rhythm to send the gondolas racing to and fro.

Centrepiece was the chair-o-plane. Single box seats attached to iron chains were strung in double rows around a central pivot flamboyantly decorated with mirrors. When the ride revolved the chairs spun out horizontally high overhead defying gravity. Girls' skirts rose provocatively and men's trilbies were tossed into the crowd.

A few days later familiar sounds – shrill organ music and thudding electricity generators – emanated from a corner of the Welfare Sports Ground at Upper Deal. Primitive communications of the 1950s are amply demonstrated here for the touring fair need move barely half a mile to attract fresh clientele. As village children we felt resentful that the mining community had so ruthlessly stolen our fair.

On rare summer evenings the front door might be prised open and Gran and I would sit side-by-side on the stone step making faces in the scudding clouds Pegasus. . . Brontosaurus. . . The Lone Ranger. . . The Tooth Fairy. . . or searching for the Evening Star. Midweek, the bell ringers would practise at St Leonard's and their uncertain peals borne on a light breeze brought treasured music. Whilst I prepared for bed, Gran would slip away quietly to catch her bus home to Deal. Inevitably, this was a time for tears.

As a child I was always scared of the dark and could sleep only with the light on in the hallway. The narrow hall was a special place of terror for me for lurking behind the hats and coats was sure to be a murderer who had lain in wait all day waiting to jump out and attack me! Frequently I cried out in the night – a request for a glass of water was always a good ploy – and once Father, exasperated by my cries, tugged me by the sleeve and shoved me out of the front door to see what terrors the dark really held.

I rose to the bait and called out in a loud voice to all the neighbours in the avenue to see what my parents had done. Lights flicked on, windows flew open. The prefab door was swiftly opened again and I was hauled in by the scruff of the neck!

For sure, Father's bedtime prayer was not designed to comfort nor console:
Matthew, Mark, Luke and John,
Bless this bed that I lie on.
Four corners to my bed.
Four angels round my head.
One to watch, one to pray,
And two to bear my soul away. . .

Generally though, I was ready to retire around eight o'clock. Changed into pyjamas, I jumped into bed with the latest Enid Blyton adventure, *The Boy Next Door,* which I read under the sheets by the light of my tri-colour torch. Father might be weeding the borders under my bedroom window and his rythmic hoe brought welcome security. Distantly, the huffing and puffing of the steam trains carrying coal from Betteshanger Colliery was a reminder that miners would be working throughout the night. Adventures of the Famous Five or Secret Seven reeled in my head as I slipped slowly into blissful oblivion. Snug as a bug in a rug.

RADIO DAYS

F RIDAY was pay day. Father would be given a special welcome when he cycled home from work pedalling furiously uphill to keep his dynamo alight. Invariably during the course of the evening – he always kept us waiting – he would produce a surprise box of chocolates or candies; Rowntree's Dairy Box, Mackintosh's Quality Street or Cadbury's Lucky Numbers.

Father still had to work on Saturdays so for him the weekend had not yet started. All the same it was a time for menfolk generally to reclaim their home and as a matter of course they would expect their wives to have a hot meal waiting on the table and their slippers warming by the fire. Father would exchange his collar and tie for a cardigan and corduroys before settling beside the fire to browse belatedly through the newspaper.

Father would also treat himself to a record from the local music store, Goulden and Wind. We watched intently as he carefully slipped the shiny record out of its brown paper sleeve and place it gently on the turntable of our obsolete 1940s Decca radiogram, which occupied one entire corner of the lounge. He would stare into space, hands cupped in ecstasy, as he played his record overandoverandover until he felt he knew all the words.

The radiogram, which incorporated radio and record player, had a bottom drawer with a rack for storing records. The turntable had a stacking system that played ten records one at a time. You had to wait until the last one was finished before turning them over to play the flip sides in reverse order. There were various speeds – 16 rpm, 33 rpm and 78 rpm – but if you accidentally

51

played the record at the wrong speed there was a dreadful wail which we found hilarious.

There were various gramophone recording companies: Parlophone, Decca, Columbia and His Master's Voice, whose label featured the terrier, Nipper, listening through the horn of a wind-up gramophone similar to the one Gran owned. Needles came in attractive little tins but they were expensive and had to be changed frequently. As a child I never could relate the placing of a record on the turntable to the voice of the artiste. I thought that somehow the singer stood in a studio by a microphone patiently awaiting your signal before starting to sing!

Dad preferred the female singers of the time. He bought their latest recording almost as soon as they appeared. Favourites were Vera Lynn, Anne Shelton, Shirley Bassey, Eve Boswell, Alma Cogan, Eartha Kitt and those darling Beverley Sisters.

Mum adored the honky tonk pianist, Russ Conway, who rose to fame on television with his friendly smile and engaging wink sideways to the cameras as he played his bouncy tune, Sidesaddle. My family loved film themes, such as Legend of The Glass Mountain and Dream of Olwyn. We whistled the tune of Perry Como's Ma-gic Mo-ments and sang along with Max Bygraves, 'You Need Hands. . .' We spurned Elvis Presley's string of rock recordings although we practically wore out Frank Sinatra's Three Coins In A Fountain. But the nearest we came to the classics was the pianist, Charlie Kunz.

There were several records which were produced exclusively for children. They captured our imagination and were repeatedly requested on children's radio programmes.

Puff the Magic Dragon, How Much Is That Doggie In the Window? Runaway Train and The Ugly Duckling sung by Danny Kaye. My favourite was Teddy Bears' Picnic, which I could recite as a party piece: 'If you go down in the woods today, you're sure of a big SURPRISE!'

There were three main radio stations: Home, Light and Third. We regarded the Home Service as rather stuffy, although it regularly produced quality plays. Newsreaders, we learned, sat at their microphones in full evening suits! How well everyone spoke in those days! *Woman's Hour* was broadcast every afternoon but preceding this was a short programme for infants, *Listen With Mother*. Rhymes and jingles were accompanied by a fairy story read by a twee lady who invariably asked: 'Are you sitting comfortably? . . . Then I'll begin.'

Francis Durbridge's convoluted Paul Temple mysteries (introduced by the dashing theme music, Coronation Scot) was far too clever for me to appreciate at that time. *Mrs Dale's Diary* ('I'm worried about Jim. . .') was a phenomenally successful weekday series and also *The Archers*, featuring the irascible Walter Gabriel, billed as an every day story of country folk. The series centred upon the fictional village of Ambridge continues to this day.

My family preferred the Light programme with its entertaining mixture of variety and comedy. Every evening there was a light hearted series which I could listen to on condition I was changed into my pyjamas. Mum threaded the elastic through the bottom of my pyjamas while my own bottom roasted by the fire. A great favourite was *Life With The Lyons* starring Ben Lyons and Bebe Daniels. But Al Read, Ted Ray and the diminutive Jimmy Clitheroe all had their own series. Later came *The Navy Lark* and *Beyond Our Ken* whose camp humour was lost for the most part on our staid family circle. Not to be missed was Wilfred Pickles' audience participation quiz show, *Have A Go*, with Mabel at the table ('How much is there in the kitty, Mabel?') In the mid 1960s this programme was broadcast live from Deal.

These shows were repeated at Sunday lunch times and we listened as a family as we tucked into our roast dinner. *Meet The Huggets* was embarrassingly

inept but *Take It From Here* featuring The Glums (Jimmy Edwards, June Whitfield and Dick Bentley) was hilarious. These comedies were preceded by *The Billy Cotton Band Show* ('Wakey, Waaaaaakey!') which we loathed. Best of all was Peter Brough's *Educating Archie*. This must be the most mystifying programme of all time since it featured ventriloquism on radio! Archie s friend might by the wonderful Beryl Reid as the naughty schoolgirl, Marlene, or Tony Hancock as his blundering tutor.

Parlour games played by celebrities were popular. *Animal Vegetable or Mineral* seemed a trifle tame compared to the raucous *Does The Team Think?* *The Brains Trust* was intensely earnest but the questions on the inter-schools challenge, *Top of the Form*, became noticeably easier as the contestants became dimmer. Oddities numbered the animal impersonations of Percy Edwards and the gobbledygook of Stanley Unwin.

There were special children's programmes introduced by Derek McCulloch. *Toytown* had a catchy tune and a wonderful cast of characters including Larry the Lamb, Dennis the Dachschund and the longsuffering Mr Mayor. Far more adventurous was *Journey Into Space* with its heroes Jet Morgan and Rocky Mountain. My great favourite was the adventures of those boy detectives, *Norman and Henry Bones*. Uncle Mac always signed off with the phrase: 'Goodnight, children . . . everywhere.'

Highlights of the week were when my two favourite comics were delivered to the door. A bonus was when they contained free gifts such as the Whiz Bang, folded paper which made a deafening crack when you whipped it, contained in *Beezer*. My preferred comics were *Dandy* which came out on Tuesdays, and better still *Beano*, on Thursdays (they cost 2d each). I was lost for hours in the company of Dennis the Menace, Beryl the Peril, Desperate Dan, Korky the Cat, Roger the Dodger, Keyhole Kate, Pansy Potter and Lord Snooty. I lay on my tummy on the half-moon hearth rug before the coal fire, legs swinging in the air, pausing to turn over when I scorched down one side.

There were more expensive comics – *Hotspur, Wizard, Topper, Swift, Robin* – but these concentrated on manly adventures rather than rip-roaring fun. Here was the world of space explorers, footballing heroes, schoolgirl detectives and jungle adventurers. Easily the most popular comic paper among boys was *Eagle* (published every Wednesday, price 4d). On the front cover was Dan Dare, Pilot of the Future; on the back was David, the Shepherd King, while in the centre were cutaway illustrations of tanks, tugs, bombers, jet planes and sports cars. I delved into such comics only when I swapped with Richard, a neighbour. He was a keen financier and drove a hard bargain, for his 'rags' cost twice mine and the pile I ended up with was miserably thin. Mother insisted that for educational purposes I studied the weekly *Children's Newspaper* whose desultory pages appealed only to swots.

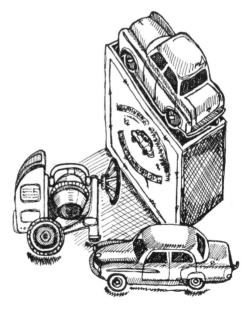

There was a dearth of books in our prefab. I cannot remember anyone in my family ever reading a borrowed book let alone buying one. A visit to the library was a rare occurrence for my parents. Probably there were a handful of Penguin paperbacks in their distinctive green (fiction) or orange (non-fiction) covers. And, yes, once, when I went rummaging under their bed, I found an illicit paperback, *Lady Chatterley's Lover.*

A few toys were saved for special occasions and might be played with only indoors. I had a wooden fort (but not enough soldiers for a battle) and a farm (the animals had wonky legs). Britains produced a miniature garden complete with metal flower beds, greenhouses and tools, which I envied, while Minic made a model harbour with ships, quays and a lighthouse.

Matchbox toys were inexpensive and finely detailed. My array of miniatures included the horse drawn milk float, a cement mixer and a dustcart. Most of my friends had an impressive collection of Dinky and Corgi toys. The latter were more desirable because they boasted the refinement of plastic windows, rubber tyres and spring suspension. Not to be left out I acquired an odd assortment: a car transporter, a horse box, a loudspeaker van and a streamlined fire engine with a ladder on top and a bell in front. For Christmases and birthdays I always requested toy lorries. This puzzled my relatives but I had made a pretend fairground with roundabouts and sideshows out of toilet rolls and cheese boxes which I used to transport from one corner of the lounge to another.

A few expensive boxed toys were reserved for playing indoors. These included chemistry, carpentry and magic sets. At family gatherings I entertained my reluctant audience with such spectacular illusions as passing a nail through my finger or bending a magic wand. Another participation game involved a bus conductor's outfit which included a machine for clipping tickets torn from rolls. Relatives and friends sat on kitchen chairs in double rows pretending to be going for a bus ride. Quite delightful were the toy post office with child's stationery, and sweet shop with tiny sweets in glass jars to be weighed on miniature scales. Generally these were shared activities. More robust playthings were Fuzzy Felt boards for making scenes from cut out felts; Potato Men with plastic features for sticking into real potatoes and cut out costumes for dressing cardboard dolls.

Perhaps the most laborious game was blow football where opponents had to steer a ping pong ball into opposite goals by blowing through a straw – difficult without a partner.

Airfix kits were popular with my practical friends. At first they were exclusive to Woolworth's. The *Golden Hind* ship model was so popular when it appeared in 1952 that it was followed soon after with the Spitfire. It was fun assembling the plastic pieces but a chore painting the completed model. Balsa wood gliders, also sold in kit form, had the advantage of actually flying.

Plaster of Paris models from rubber moulds also needed to be painted by hand. Other artistic toys were stencils, transfers and gummed shapes. Jigsaws involved the whole family and sticking cut-out scraps into scrapbooks with flour and water paste kept me quiet for hours. There was a craze for painting by numbers in the 1950s, among both children and adults, and the artistic results were sometimes framed and displayed on prefab walls.

Everyone collected something so there was always an opportunity for swaps. Beer mats and matchboxes were the prized collections but there were also postcards, badges, foreign coins and stamps. Girls collected buttons, pebbles and beads which they displayed in their fathers' discarded tobacco tins. Weedy kids made a collection of cheese labels but gathered few admirers.

Stamp collecting has never lost its appeal. Like millions of kids today I bought a starter pack of assorted used stamps from around the world and proceeded to sort them before sticking them into an album. Members of the family puzzled over some of the strange names of countries that issued pictorial stamps – Duttia, Helvetia, Sverige, Gwalior, Bussahir, Orange Free State . . . Quite attractive were the British commemoratives, then in their infancy: The

Festival of Britain, Sixth British Empire and Commonwealth Games, World Scout Jubilee Jamboree and a set of British castles which included Dover Castle atop the White Cliffs. Avidly, I awaited the Christmas mail from relatives in New Zealand. These stamps carried exquisite Nativity scenes.

Our family settled down in front of the fire most winter evenings to play a choice of games. Compendium sets comprised Snakes and Ladders, Draughts, Dominoes, Ludo and Tiddlywinks. Cards were never played in our home, possibly because of our Baptist influence. A type of card game our family did indulge in, however, was called Pitt. This was based on the American wheat market and involved noisy bartering that culminated in chaos. Beetle drives were compulsory at family gatherings and also Housey-Housey, which was the forerunner of the Bingo craze that swept the country in the 1960s.

One educational toy was the Magic Robot. A question posed to this minute oracle was answered with a wave of his wand indicating the correct answer on a set of cards. He was operated by means of a concealed magnet. Another favourite was a tiny tin magic lantern which came complete with several celluloid strips of slides. These were projected onto one wall of our lounge where Mum had thoughtfully pinned a miniature screen. I was quite imaginative when making up the accompanying stories despite being hampered by not recognising a single character among the illuminated cartoons.

Father made me a portable puppet booth so that I could entertain the neighbours at parties. It was a terrific affair with pull-along red velvet curtains, wooden rods to hold my painted scenery and a miniature stage for the properties. Unfortunately all the hand puppets were inferior items won at the fair.

They had cheap chalk heads with garish painted faces and none of the characters seemed to relate. Nevertheless I put on a grand performance both as presenter and puppeteer in the manner of Harry Corbett with his rascally glove puppets, Sooty, Sue and Sweep. 'Izzy, wizzy, let's get bizzy.'

Eventually I progressed to marionettes. The first I owned was a heavy metal puppet called the Turnip Man which may have been a television character. A more charming puppet was Little White Bull which featured in a film starring Tommy Steele. Pelham Puppets were the pinnacle of marionette makers. I saved and saved until I could afford them – they were so inventive: Big Bad Wolf, a wicked witch, an ogre, a negro minstrel, a schoolmaster in cap and gown, a tortoise in a duffel coat . . . I have some of these puppets today still in their original boxes.

Nonconformist chapels which Gran attended regularly were far from sombre for they provided welcome entertainment in those dark days after the war. The Methodist Hall was the scene of an extraordinary spectacle which I can remember only vaguely. A Parade of Queens consisted of sovereigns from the past completing a circuit of the hall with their shaky crowns and retinue while the audience sang patriotic songs. There seemed an endless succession – Mary Tudor, Elizabeth I, Queen Anne – but what the exact purpose was no one can recall. Perhaps it was the Coronation?

One winter the Congregationalist Chapel (distinguished by its twin spires) presented Tableaux. This puzzling form of entertainment must surely hark back to Victorian times. The idea was that actors stood like statues to represent scenes from the past while a narrator read from a storybook. The theme was to be the Biblical love story of Ruth and Boaz. Gran was cast as Naomi. For weeks we hunted out properties and costume. There were no lines to be learned, luckily, for no-one was permitted to speak.

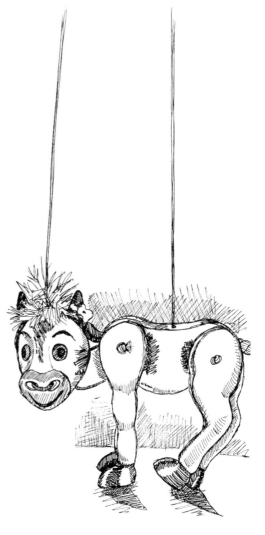

When the great day came Mum and I secured our seats in the front row. The green baize curtains were swished aside to reveal a colourful Egyptian scene on the dais. Against a painted backcloth of pyramids Gran sat at a spinning wheel while her daughter, Ruth, still wearing her spectacles, bade her farewell. She was going to marry Boaz who was played by a portly matron sporting a false beard. The text was read, the scene over, the curtains were drawn and the characters were gone forever. There was thunderous applause. We were proud of Gran. She hadn't moved an inch.

Television came late to Carter Avenue. The Dry family at

Number 10 acquired one in the mid 1950s. Mr Dry was a Royal Navy seaman and so could afford to buy one for his large family. All boys.

We noticed that about nine months after each home leave Mrs Dry produced yet another offspring. This was mystifying. However, since Mr Dry was far from home at the time of the new baby's arrival we surmised that it could have nothing to do with him.

The Drys welcomed everyone in to stare at their minute screen – just a thought, but did they build it themselves from components? We all took a chair and a mug for our complimentary tea. After an hour's viewing of *Children's Hour* I used to make my exit with that rehearsed speech: 'Thank you very much for having me and I hope I can come again.' One day the room went silent as I was in full flow and it slowly dawned on me that my studied politeness was being mocked!

Television was broadcast late in the afternoon and initially there was a break between six and seven o'clock to allow for children to be put to bed. Once you switched on you had to wait ages for the set to warm up, when there was a slight smell of burning dust. The picture was much dimmer than it is today and electrical interference resulting in a snowy screen was caused by passing cars, or even a neighbour hoovering. There was only one channel at first – BBC – and programmes were screened in black and white. Colour television was something we dreamed about but at the time seemed most unlikely to happen in our lifetime. Three-colour filters could be fitted to the screen by

suction pads, making the lower third of the screen green (for grass), the middle third pink (for flesh tones) and the top third blue (for sky). By the end off the decade H- or X-shaped television aerials were hoisted above every prefab. Home life in Carter Avenue had changed forever.

Children's Hour began our day's viewing. That insufferable Annette Mills sang sweetly to Muffin the Mule as he clip-clopped along on the lid of her upright piano. You could see the strings. Puppets were thought to be the ideal entertainment for children. Perhaps they were for as infants we all followed the antics of The Woodentops, Rag, Tag and Bobtail, Andy Pandy and Loopy Loo, Bill and Ben and Little Weed. Later we progressed in humour to Terry Hall with Lenny the Lion and Shari Lewis with Lamb Chop.

Legendary heroes were the subjects of smashing children's serials: Robin Hood, Ivanhoe and William Tell. Even Jesus of Nazareth and Paul of Tarsus could still muster an army of fans on Sunday afternoons. There was the serialisation of classics such as *The Black Arrow* and *The Black Tulip*, but my special favourite was the American adventures of Circus Boy. More practically we copied the illustrations of Tony Hart; listened to the yarns of Johnny Morris, the hot chestnut man, and chortled at the antics of Mr Pastry. Eamonn Andrews was the stilted host of *Crackerjack* featuring a competition for kids, Double or Drop (three cabbages and you were out of the game).

Television was live in the days before video recording. A play would have continuous action which meant that if an actor had to dodge from one part of the set to another a second actor would be given extra lines to cover until that character arrived, sometimes with a change of clothing and always out of breath. Outside broadcasting was kept to a minimum and so scenery inevitably appeared studio-bound. I remember actors bouncing up and down on the seats of a stationary bus to create the illusion of movement against an unconvincing back projection of a busy road.

61

Westerns were screened nightly: *Wells Fargo, Wyatt Earp, Laramie, Maverick, Gunsmoke, Wagon Train Cisci Kid, Rawhide* ('Rolling, rolling, rolling, keep those doggies moving . . . Head 'em up, move 'em out . . .') Wildlife programmes were introduced by David Attenborough and underwater adventures featured Hans and Lotte Hass. American crooners like Perry Como hosted their own variety shows but British comedy series still harked back to the war with *The Army Game*, starring that incomparable pair, Bootsie and Snudge.

Dixon of Dock Green was a firm favourite on Saturday evenings. It always ended with Jack Warner as PC George Dixon, the kindly village bobby, saluting and saying: 'Goodnight all.' Often he forgot his lines and you could distinctly hear the prompter. Mother's hearthrob, Andy Crawford, CID, was eventually killed in the line of duty having defected to ITV.

Comedians we adored were Frankie Howerd, Arthur Askey, Eric Sykes and Professor Jimmie Edwards, the rascally headmaster in *Whacko!* Everything stopped for Anthony Aloysious Hancock of 22, Railway Cuttings, East Cheam. He was the first comedian to make the switch from radio to television and the twenty-five minutes of *Hancock's Half Hour,* co-starring wily partner Sid James, was sheer magic. Charlie Drake was desperately funny in those days and his knockabout routines positively dangerous. Once he was pulled

through a packed bookcase and failed to reappear the other side. The screen went blank and we learned from the papers the next day he had knocked himself out and had been taken to hospital, unconscious.

Viewing was often disrupted through a technical fault or atmospheric conditions, particularly in the summer months. Cards with printed apologies were screened: DO NOT ADJUST YOUR SET or NORMAL SERVICE WILL BE RESUMED AS SOON AS POSSIBLE. At such times music was played with short films of a potter's wheel, waves crashing or kittens playing, thought to soothe our nerves. When ITV appeared, if there were a break in the film they simply abandoned the ending and dived straight into the adverts. Most disconcerting.

We must have been the last family to have ITV. Southern Television commenced in 1960 but before then London ITV could be received by people who hired Rediffusion. Mother in any case thought ITV vulgar because of the commercials (she even kept the *Radio Times* discreetly in a decorated leather cover). This meant that I was always mystified at school when programmes such as *Double Your Money* and *Criss Cross Quiz* were mentioned by playmates. I felt left out, too, when everyone repeated catch phrases or chanted advert jingles. 'A Mars a day helps you work, rest and play.' 'Don't forget the fruit gums, Mum.' 'Hoover – it beats as it sweeps as it cleans.' 'I d love a Babycham.' 'Hands that do dishes can feel soft as your face.' 'You ll wonder where the yellow went when you clean your teeth with Pepsodent.' The very first televised commercial was for 'tingling Gibbs SR'.

Then again we had been the last to have a television in our avenue. My parents had even pondered whether they could afford the £2 licence fee (£1 for sound only). When they finally bought a set it was our pride and joy. They had experimented with a Philips, a Bush, a PYE and an EKCO but settled on a Decca console with tambour doors concealing the bulbous screen during the daytime. Everyone envied us. Our television cabinet had a mammoth 17 inch screen!

By then my family was hooked on television. We tried to limit viewing to a few hours every night and Father refused permission for us to eat pre-packed television dinners on trays in front of the screen. We were careful never to watch television in the dark as this was sure to damage our eyes. Also we were firmly polite in turning off the television whenever visitors arrived – something which not all our neighbours did!

But in reality we watched almost everything through to *The Epilogue,* The Queen and the disappearing dot on a blank screen round about midnight.

Even so the focus of our room instantly changed (as it did in every home across Britain) from the coal fire in the centre of the lounge to the gogglebox in the corner. Winter evenings were never the same. Mum was thrilled when Pearl Carr and Teddy Johnson won the Eurovision Song Contest, with Sing Little Birdie, while Dad had difficulty in deciding which glamourous model would win the Miss World title: 'It'll be Miss Paraguay . . . definitely. Or it could be Miss Brazil . . . no, wait, just look at Miss Ceylon.'

Gran appreciated *The Good Old Days* which transported her back to Edwardian times, while the whole family revelled in the Brian Rix Farces televised direct from the Whitehall Theatre.

We relished panel games like *What's My Line?* with the stylish Lady Isobel

Barnett, the cantankerous Gilbert Harding and the wry Cyril Fletcher. Quiz shows were *Double Your Money,* with Hughie Green, and *Take Your Pick*, with Michael Miles, where contestants had to decide whether to open the magical box 13. Once a honeymoon couple were sent to New York to collect a rolling pin! One programme which has never lost its impact in the opening moments is *This Is Your Life* (hosted by Eamonn Andrews). People surprised were not just pop stars and television celebs but folk who had led worthwhile lives, such as the missionary, Gladys Aylward, and the wartime pilot, Douglas Bader.

Adult series numbered *The Third Man, Probation Officer, No Hiding Place, The Plane Makers, Knight Errant, Cannonball, Bonanza, Interpol Calling* and *The Four Just Men.* Perry Mason's complicated courtroom dramas always ended with the murderer – the least likely suspect – breaking down and confessing in the witness box. Francis Durbridge's mystery thrillers successfully transferred from radio to television and included *The World of Tim Fraser* and *The Scarf.* We laughed at the antics of Peggy Mount and David Kossoff as the irrepressible country family, *The Larkins,* and adored the American comedienne, Lucille Ball, in her interminable series, *I Love Lucy.* And for variety we mustn't forget the high-kicking Television Toppers on *The Black and White Minstrel Show* nor the challenging games on Beat the Clock, compered by Bruce 'I'm in charge' Forsythe, half way through *Sunday Night At The London Palladium*.

Alternative entertainment was still a visit to the 'flicks'. Deal had three cinemas – Regent, Royal and Odeon – which changed their programmes twice weekly. I was an avid picturegoer and watched intently as the managers displayed new posters in their NOW SHOWING frames and altered the stills boards to advertise FORTHCOMING ATTRACTIONS. Popular movies took months to arrive and with the advent of James Bond blockbusters there were extensive queues when fans were sometimes turned away disappointed.

Patrons certainly received good value. Apart from the main feature there was a second film and a full programme of cartoons, trailers, documentaries, Pathé news and Pearl and Dean advertisements. Inevitably there were tedious war reels and dubious naturist shorts with bare-breasted females playing tennis in longshot. The B movies were often hugely entertaining – an Edgar Wallace mystery or a Boulting Brothers comedy. British films were well supported and popular stars appeared in repertory – Peter Sellers, Ian Carmichael, Terry Thomas, James Robertson Justice.

The first film mother took me to was *Reach For The Sky*, the filmed biography of Douglas Bader, the legless pilot, starring Kenneth Moore. From then onwards I was hooked and I would sneak into a cinema at every opportunity. Favourite films were the musicals, *High Society* and *The Wizard Of Oz*, and spectacular adventures with special effects recreating prehistoric monsters, Jules Verne's *Journey To The Centre of the Earth* and Conan Doyle's *The Lost World*. Classics included *The Inn of the Sixth Happiness*, *The Nun's Story* and *A Night To Remember*, telling the story of the sinking of RMS *Titanic*. Patriotic war films numbered *From Here To Eternity*, *The Wooden Horse*, *The Man Who Never Was*, *The Bridge On The River Kwai* and *The Dam Busters* with its stirring theme music. The 1950s heralded the advent of the interminable Carry On and Doctor series.

Cecil B de Mille produced the most spectacular biblical epics including *Ben Hur*, featuring that stupendous chariot race, and a monumental *The Ten Commandments*, miraculously filming Moses' parting of the Red Sea. Walt Disney, who continues to entrance whole generations of children, produced such wonderful animated films as *Lady and The Tramp, Pinnochio, Cinderella* and *Bambi*. The unruly Carter Avenue gang were held spellbound by *Snow White*. We occupied an entire row of tip-up seats and wandered home in a crocodile line imitating the seven dwarfs by singing 'Heigh, ho! Heigh, ho! It's off to work we go . . .'

Stage musicals – The *King and I, The Boy Friend, Kismet, Calamity Jane, Gigi, Guys and Dolls, My Fair Lady* and *West Side Story* – eventually made their way onto the big screen. My cousin and I watched *South Pacific* one hot summer afternoon at The Royal. We were so disgusted at having to sit through sixteen songs that we imperiously demanded our money back. When mother took me to my first live musical, *The Sound of Music*, in London's West End sometime in the 1960s, we sat so high up in the gods we could peer over the cardboard mountains behind which the Von Trapp family were climbing ladders backstage to escape from the Nazis.

Most films were in black and white so it was a real treat when the main feature advertised 'glorious Technicolor'. Innovations also included 3D, stereophonic sound and Cinemascope. There were often hitches during the screening. The film might break down or there would be a power failure. Once the reels were mixed up and shown in reverse order during a thriller so that we found out who was the villain before the deed was done!

Gran was an ardent film fan. Rain or shine she would go the pictures two or three times a week. There were continuous performances so she would watch the main feature three times over while other people left at the point where they recognised they had come in. Half way through, one of her friends would arrive with refreshments – a flask of soup and some sandwiches – and the pair would sit munching away, enjoying the warmth and comfort and escapism of the cinema until the ruched curtain finally descended.

Encouraged by Gran, I defied my parents by seeing four different films at The Royal in one week! It was a special Dickens Festival and so I returned on alternate nights to watch the 1940's black and white classics: *Great Expectations, Oliver Twist, Nicholas Nickleby* and *A Tale of Two Cities*. I sniffled with sympathy when Dirk Bogarde, as Sidney Carlton, gave up his life for a friend on the guillotine, and reeled in horror as the unscrupulous Ralph Nickleby swung by his neck from the staircase to avoid arrest by the bobbies. Scenery in these films was always stagey and I was conscious that I was watching an outmoded style of acting reminiscent of Victorian theatre.

Flicking though the pages of *PictureGoer* or listening to the radio's *Movie Go Round*, we ardently followed the careers of our idols – Gregory Peck, Grace Kelly, Sophia Loren, Marilyn Monroe, James Stewart, Doris Day, Jayne Mansfield, Cary Grant, Bette Davis, Herbert Lom, Charlton Heston, Victor Mature, Audrey Hepburn. Our unruffled heroes, it seems, were always suited and hatted while our tantalising heroines were dumb blondes with dainty hats and white gloves. Even when experiencing darkest danger solely for our entertainment.

Contemporary films struck a strong note of sentimentality which has certainly passed into the realm of cinema history. There were three categories of films: U for universal entertainment; A for more daring films to which children were admitted only when accompanied by an adult and X-rated films that were violent or mildly erotic. Moviemakers experimented with more spectacular devices to attract dwindling audiences. There were special cellophane spectacles – one lens red and the other green – which gave a three-dimensional effect and another time similar cardboard specs were provided so that spooks appeared in a creepy film only when patrons peered through the lenses.

There were frequent intervals while the projectionist changed the reels and during the intermission an usherette would sell ice cream and popcorn from her tray by the light of her torch. Courting couples shared twin seats at the back of the auditorium and there was always a mad scramble to leave the cinema before the screening of the National Anthem. My parents were politely patriotic so we stood for The Queen before searching for our hats and gloves under the tip-up seats and then walked out smartly into the street still living the film.

SATURDAY SIXPENCE

S ATURDAYS always had a lazy start for my family. Mother was an infant teacher and I was a pupil at the nearby primary school so this was our first opportunity to lie-in during a busy week. I used to sneak in to my parents' bedroom to watch Father struggling to fix a freshly starched collar to his cotton work shirt after hunting for a stud on the utility dressing table. Brand new shirts might herald disaster, for they arrived in boxes and their packaging included thin cardboard, tissue paper and masses of pins, one of which was sure to be left in when you put the shirt on. Ouch! Once dressed, Dad would push out his Raleigh from the shed and return while wrestling with his cycle clips to give me my pocket money – the treasured Saturday Sixpence.

Decimal coinage was introduced in 1971. How Gran struggled to comprehend it! To me it always seemed so logical and simple – one hundred pennies equal one pound. Pounds, shillings and pence, £sd, which it replaced, was the bane of my early life, particularly at school where it took ages to add up sums involving money. Pennies were called coppers and bore a large portrait of one of the sovereigns. You were as likely to carry a coin with the head of Victoria draped in widow's weeds as you were to find a profile of our young Queen with her hair tied in ribbons. The reverse of all pennies featured Britannia with her trident, helmet and shield. Twelve pennies made one shilling, two hundred and forty made one pound.They weighed a ton. A pile made a hole in your pocket. But if you jiggled them around you certainly felt rich.

In addition there were half-pennies and farthings. A farthing, valued at a quarter of one penny, was the smallest coin in currency and it carried a picture of the smallest British bird, a wren. There was precious little you could buy with this coin, sweets, mainly, but bus fares were often calculated to the near-

est farthing.

Brass threepenny bits were attractive twelve-sided coins bearing either a sprig of clover or a portcullis. Silver coinage comprised a sixpence, known as a tanner; one shilling, a bob and two shillings, a florin. Half-a-crown was the princely tip if relatives stayed but, apart from a special commemorative mintage, there was no such thing as a crown in the 1950s. Ten shillings and one pound were paper currency. Shop goods were craftily priced in guineas – £1 1s. It was hoped that customers would not notice the additional shillings, which soon mounted up. Another annoying trick was that items were priced £1 19s 11d. In other words one penny less than the next pound. Somehow it looked far less!

Father worked in the Co-Operative, a large L-shaped store in the centre of the town which sold everything from linoleum to lingerie. He was the under manager, waged at £5 per week. The store specialised in reasonably priced furnishings for newly-married couples . . . but it also dealt in funerals. When the manager was absent drumming up trade from recently bereaved families father was put in charge of the store. Once he had to discipline five mischievous salesgirls who were entertaining customers in the fashion department with a demonstration of the jitterbug.

A feature of Deal's Co-Op was the cash railway. Once a purchase had been made, the sales assistant placed the money in a wooden cup which was then screwed into a container high above the counter. By means of a spring lever the container was then catapulted along overhead wires to the cashier in a central pay desk. Customers waited patiently for their change to be returned in the same novel manner.

Traditional cooked breakfasts went out of fashion in the Fifties – mainly because most women worked – but Mum generally managed fried eggs as a Saturday treat. Sunny side up. Or a boiled egg with toasted soldiers. My job was to toast thick slices of Hovis on the two-bar electric fire which we stood on the kitchen table, oblivious to safety. Mum read *The Sketch* (Dad would already have cut out the pin-up girl) and when she had finished I perused the cartoons: Tug Transon, Peanuts, The Gambols, Pop and Blondie.

My world had been shattered one afternoon as I arrived home from school to find Mum barring the front door (rarely used) and saying: 'Wait 'til your father gets home. There's a surprise inside. Just for you.' I'd never before had a surprise so I was instantly suspicious and, indeed, I've hated surprises ever since.

My worst fears were realised the moment the door was flung open to reveal an upright piano at the far end of the lounge – a gift from the relatives in Derby. There it stood, two wonky candle sconces aside a central music stand

71

with the lid propped open to display its yellowing ivory keys. A monstrous smiling use.

Mother had great expectations for me as a concert pianist. Father more realistically ventured that perhaps one day I might earn a few pints playing at the local pub. At once I saw the years of misery that lay ahead. Practising The Piano. This dread was instantly confirmed when my gang appeared, swaying on the garden fence, a football under our captain's arm, waving wildly through the window, as I tentatively tried the keys.

Music lessons were inevitably on a Saturday morning. Each week I took my place alongside demure pupils who sat in silence on three sides of the front parlour awaiting tuition by Mrs Mynot. Our teacher always sat alongside you as you played, her straight back never touching the chair, so that she could press the pedals if you couldn't quite reach. To beat time – and lazy pupils – she kept a wooden ruler lodged behind those menacing black notes. Eyes on the music, eyes on the ruler, never on the keys . . . THWACK!

The first manuscript I remember was by Rene Storm which had alternate pages to be played by alternate hands. Inspiring titles included *A Rainy Day* and *At The Zoo*. Even now I shudder at the thought of crochets, quavers, minims, semi-breves and inaccessible scales which my infant fingers refused to reach. But how proud mother was the first time I belted out *Greensleeves*.

Bread and butter before jelly and ice cream was always the golden rule of children's tea parties. So once the misery of music had been endured there was a wonderful treat in store . . . week by blissful week. Saturday Morning Cinema. Yippee!

Deal's Odeon Cinema was an apology for an Art Deco building. It had a plain white rendered frontage with an awning over the entrance and rows of stills boards advertising the current adult films – *Circus of Horrors, Godzilla, King Kong, The Fly* – beneath a tall tower which appeared to have no particular purpose. Excited children entered through the middle of the auditorium where aproned usherettes tore tickets and divided them with the beam of their torches: 6d for the stalls or 1/- for the circle (that extra tanner provided access to an additional vantage point for raining down ammunition – empty ice cream tubs – after the interval)

There was immediate hush once the auditorium darkened and the ruched curtain rose to reveal the weekly fare of cartoons, serials and features. Batman and Robin, those caped crusaders – POW! – provided intense excitement – WHAM! – as they underwent perilous predicaments – ZAP! Each week there was a cliffhanger where they were left in seemingly dire straights – bound and gagged and held over myriad spikes; bound and gagged beneath an avalanche of crashing boulders; bound and gagged in a bare room where the walls were fast closing in . . . FIND OUT NEXT WEEK! We were left to ponder in agony for a further seven days as to how they could possibly make their escape. But with one bound they were free . . . only to encounter further catastrophes all in the cause of justice.

The interval was heralded by the arrival of the usherettes with trays of lollies, ice cream cones and mint chocbars. On the rare occasions when I had spare cash I treated myself to popcorn or a bag of crisps. Smith's crisps provided salt in blue twists hidden at the bottom of the bag. Sometimes you got so lost in the film that you found yourself chewing them in mistake for crisps! The interval was always the chance to creep up to an empty seat in the more expensive circle. Or set off stink bombs in the crowded auditorium.

During the interval the management provided entertainment live on stage to distract us from fighting. Skiffle groups were all the rage in the Fifties. Once a trio of talentless teddy boys played a guitar, a washboard (a thimble for a plectrum) and a double bass comprising a packing case with a broom handle and thick cord. They crooned the current hits: Lonnie Donegan's *My Old Man's A Dustman*, Joe Brown's *Knees Up Muvver Brown* and Bill Hailey and The Comets' *Rock Around The Clock,* accompanied by one thousand screaming kids attempting to hand jive.

Teddy boys were dressed in electric blue or plum red knee-length jackets

with velvet collars (drapes), bootlace ties, drainpipe trousers and thick crepe-soled shoes called brothel creepers. Teds had greased hair in the form of a quiff and long sideburns. Their girlfriends wore circle skirts, bobby socks and pony tails. One notorious gang hung out at Gabriel's Italian Coffee Bar in our High Street where their motorbikes and Lambrettas permanently obstructed the pavement. They crowded around the American jukebox, listening to hit singles while sipping espresso coffee served from a satanically hissing urn.

At The Odeon, full length feature films especially made for children included *Greyfriars Bobby*, *The Red Balloon* and *Whistle Down The Wind*. Cartoons were perennially popular, especially Bugs Bunny, Tom and Jerry, Goofy and Woody Woodpecker. We cheered such diverse heroes as Tarzan, Zorro, Flash Gordon and Lassie. One week the film featured Davy Crockett. My gang copied this hero by sporting imitation raccoon hats with stripy tails and charging round the prefabs chanting:

 'Dav-y, Davy Crockett,
 King of the wild front-ier!'

As I had missed the screening, due to chicken pox or measles, I was never sure who Dav-y was, or where the wild frontier, but I still joined in with gusto.

Most popular were westerns. Cowboys and their horses were the masked Lone Ranger (Silver) Hopalong Cassidy (Topper) Gene Autry (Champion) and Roy Rogers with his performing palomino, Trigger, billed as The Smartest Horse in the Movies. Incongruously, several of these tough heroes were liable to burst into song while alone on the prairie at night with just the stars and a full orchestra. These touching moments brought forth catcalls from the young audience impatient for action.

Film directors managed with skilful ingenuity to ring the changes week-by-week but the ingredients were always the same: Dodge City . . . bank robberies . . . jail breaks . . . saloon bars . . . gun duels . . . gold mines . . . rodeos . . . wagon trains . . . Wells Fargo stage coaches. (Why did the wheels always turn backwards?) Here was a rare chance for audience participation. The whole cinema roared as the cowboys (Hurrah!) chased the Injuns (Boo!) faster and faster across the dusty wide screen. All was resolved – totally unfairly – when the cavalry appeared blaring trumpets on the distant horizon (Hurrah! Hurrah!) And as the heroes rode into the sunset we charged into the sunlight where a posse of mums were rounding up their kids to take them back to the ranch.

My mother was always the last. She arrived, huffing and puffing, laden with her empty bucket shopping basket. No matter how long she spent in the town Mum's deep leather bag rarely held more than two or three items. As a local teacher, she was well-known and well-liked, so everyone, it seemed, wanted to chat to her. Reluctantly, I was dragged around the shops to catch up on bargains and gossip, gossip and bargains . . .

Deal's High Street, prior to pedestrianisation, was a hive of commerce. The street was jammed by vans; the pavement blocked by prams. Boys on delivery bikes with wicker baskets weaved between the two. There were few chain stores but numerous thriving small family businesses priding themselves on 'personal and efficient service'.

Together, we might visit Crump's the confectioner, where the kindly owner weighed out loose sweets from glass jars on brass scales before scooping them into paper bags which he sealed with a deft twist . . . or Goymer's the greengrocer, a double-fronted Georgian shop on the seafront, where fruit and vegetables were displayed in one window, cocker spaniel puppies for sale in the other . . . or the wool shop that even today retains its curved chrome facade, bentwood chairs and apple wood counters containing needles, patterns, cards of buttons and plastic darning mushrooms.

After Mother had made her purchase I knew it would be my task that evening to hold the skein of wool, arms outstretched, while she laboriously wound it into a plump ball before popping into a Bakelite beehive holder ready for knitting.

Yet this shop held a certain magic for me, simply because the wooden reels of cottons and packets of embroidery silks were arranged in permutations of colour. The austerity years immediately after the Second World War drew a

veil of monochrome over our enclosed world. Television, newspapers, photographs and even children's books were all produced in stark black and white. We had to wait until the next decade before Hardy Amies' tinted pink and blue shirts added a bright splash to men's clothing.

Riceman's was our largest store, spread over several floors and linking two main streets – High Street and Queen Street. An extension was built in the late 1950s and the opening ceremony was performed by a local lad, Norman Wisdom, accompanied by his mother who, contemporary newspapers reported, 'liked shopping'. On the day when a cramped lift was installed Gran took me for thrilling vertical rides by convincing the bell boy we were extravagant customers requiring goods from several departments.

The top floor was devoted to millinery. Hats decorated with fruit, feathers and tantalising veils were grouped according to shade on short wooden stands with padded tops. It was wonderful entertainment peering in the gilded oval mirrors to watch the town's elegant ladies try on those outlandish styles. It was far more fun, in fact, than the children's corner, with its seasonal attractions – the aptly named Santa s Grotto, the tawdry in-store railway or the touring menagerie (of which I saw precious few live exhibits because I dare not pass the tank of snakes!).

Riceman's menagerie, which exhibited bears, monkeys, birds, a chimpanzee, a kangaroo and two pythons, was intended to advertise the arrival of Chipperfield's circus that winter at Victoria Park. It was an eventful season – Father Christmas was thrown from a camel which he rode triumphantly into town and the pair of pythons escaped overnight into rolls of carpet stored in the adjacent home furnishings department.

Every so often mother took me to Riceman's shoe department for a pair of despised, hard-wearing, sensible Clarks shoes. The smart assistant made you put your feet into a machine while X-rays were passed through to check that the shoes fitted perfectly and wouldn't damage healthy feet. Expediently, these gimmicky Pedoscopes were withdrawn at the end of the decade because of concerns over radiation.

If we felt flush we might join Dad for lunch. Catt's Restaurant was a popular rendezvous and lunchtime queues stretched around the corner past its own enticing bakery. My parents invariably opted for roast of the day (2/3d) while I tucked into my favourite egg on chips (1/9d) followed by Wonder Cake (8d a slice) The decor was extremely modern – Formica topped square tables, white wood chairs, plastic droplights and a colourful mural depicting a woodland glade. If only my prefab were as exotic as this . . .

By now the shiny silver sixpence would be burning a hole in the pocket of my gaberdine raincoat. At last we arrived at Woolworth's - a vast, gloomy, rambling store in the High Street.

We would fight our way past the Speak Your Weight machine and along the crowded aisles bounded by high mahogany counters selling everything from dowdy children's clothes to gaudy plastic flowers.

The toy counter at the far end stocked a trillion treasures all within my price range. There were kaleidoscopes, cowboy hats, bird whistles, skipping ropes, jigsaw puzzles, building blocks, spud guns, plasticine strips, pistols which fired strips of caps and packs of alphabet letters in bright colours . . . It was no use mum trying to hurry me by trying to choose for me – this moment was the highlight of the week.

Popular plastic toys included a pencil sharpener in the shape of a crocodile with snapping jaws; zoo animals which waddled comically down a slope; a playable trumpet in garish colours and a tiny camera with rotating views that came into focus when you clicked the shutter. Artistic materials numbered a double sided slate with coloured chalks; a sketch pad with an instant wipe-clean surface and a 'magic' painting book whose colours appeared miraculously when daubed with plain water from a brush.

There were more expensive toys, naturally, but they could only be afforded whenever rich relatives tipped that half-a-crown or by being good for an impossibly long period of time. There were streamlined metal seaplanes; a clockwork tinplate submarine, *Nautilus,* from the film *20,000 Leagues Under The Sea* and plastic versions of the stylish Cunard liners (*Queen Mary* with three funnels/*Queen Elizabeth* with two) which crossed and recrossed my bathtub in imitation of their Atlantic sailings.

Clutching my prized purchase and Mum's hand I was steered through the narrow streets to Gran's old dark house in Middle Street behind the seafront where I played contentedly while mother fell asleep in a battered armchair in the sunny sitting room. Mother was expected to run a home in addition to her school teaching so this crafty snooze was well deserved before she returned alone to our prefab. It shames me to reflect the impossible demands made on career women in post war Britain.

While Mum slept before leaving for home Gran might also take me into the town shopping. She would need help in carrying her wicker basket. The Co-op food hall was generally her first stop. She would perch on one of the high bentwood chairs, hand a list to Roy, the bespectacled and aproned assistant, and watch him dodge between the counters counting, weighing, wrapping . . . Peeping over the marble counter I could see my distorted reflection in the polished brass Imperial weights. Gran handed over her ration book for the appropriate section to be snipped out or crossed off. Butter, cheese, meat, tea and sugar were all rationed until 1954.

I might be sent alone to smaller stores nearby on errands. 'Be sure to check your change.' Every penny counted. Waste not, want not. Scrimp and save. There was Harris Mayes, the butcher's, whose floor was covered in sawdust to soak up the blood from the carcasses. Butchers never handled money but gave you a receipt for payment at the cash desk where the girl spiked your bill before allowing you to retrieve your meat. There was Lipton's, Timothy White's and The World's Stores whose tiled walls were decorated with exotic animals and birds. And there was Mrs Crew's general stores in which the only visible item in the window for sale was potatoes. Sympathetic shop-keepers realised that times were hard and offered free credit to their regular customers but less scrupulous dealers pinned a black list of folk who owed them money to their shop door or window.

Old Mrs Smith ran a secondhand shop on the corner of Farrier Street. Optimistically, it was termed a Wardrobe Dealer's. Ancient garments were strung three to a hanger from the ceiling; musty books were piled high on the doorstep while the window displays consisted of cracked mirrors, piano sconces, gold spectacles, false teeth and dead flies. So eccentric were these displays that at one time there appeared to be offered for sale a secondhand shroud! Discerning customers, however, might spot that valuable antique amongst the bric-a-brac.

Grandma rented out her attic – three cramped rooms with violently sloping ceilings reached via rickety stairs – to a young newly-wed couple. John was a corporal in the Royal Marines then stationed at Deal; Joyce was a colourist at Stewart Dunn's photographic laboratory. In the 1950s all photographs were developed in black and white. For coloured pictures you had to describe the scene to a colourist who would then tint your photographs by hand with inks. The process was expensive and only half satisfactory since much of the colouring was left to the artist's imagination.

Joyce was a kindly girl who took time to teach me the hand jive. She was fashionably dressed with a speckled batwing spectacles, a chunky woollen sweater and a pleated skirt. Painted nails and a pony tail completed her modern image. Saturday evenings Gran provided tea on a wooden tray which I carried carefully up the steep stairs to Joyce's flat to watch television. The main attraction was ITV. (At that time it was the poorer folk who had access to ITV because they rented their sets from Rediffusion whereas we owned our set but were limited at first to BBC.)

Perhaps these early evening shows were unsuitable for young people – mother certainly thought so – but it was great fun to watch them in the comfort of Joyce's cramped flat. We relished tense serials such as *The Invisible Man, The Assassin* and the Chinese detective, *Charlie Chan.* This was also my introduction to American television – the amusing escapades of *Sergeant Bilko* and the exciting police dramas, *Highway Patrol* and *Dragnet.* Further excitement came from those helicopter heroes, *Whirlybirds,* and the Australian series, *Flying Doctor.*

Adverts were still a novelty. Gloved and hatted housewives pranced around pastel shaded 'dream kitchens'. Adoring mums slaved over hot stoves to feed their appreciative family. We followed avidly antics of the Oxo family, Philip and Katy, and admired the catchy tunes advertising detergents (Persil, Surf, Daz, Omo). Or Dettol, Esso Blue, Knight's Castile and fabulous Pink Camay. There was the exultant 'aa - aa - aah Bisto' (gravy granules) and the whispered 'BO' (Lifebuoy soap). Strange, too, how these adverts affected our dialogue: nugget became 'noo-gah'; margarine became 'mah-garine' and I stopped asking for 'nice' biscuits when I learned they came from Nice.

Early evening it would be time to return to the prefab estate. Gran held my hand as we walked smartly along Middle Street, the fishermen's quarter which has now become a desirable Conservation Area.

During the war the south end of Middle Street had been heavily shelled. Rubble was piled high over the site of demolished Georgian buildings but we could still follow the road which forked before we reached the bus station. Gran would stop and call down to a woman who lived in the basement of her bombed house. She'd chat, briefly, and walk on. Strange now to think there was no house above this basement, just rubble strewn with fireweed and buddleia. Yet the woman continued to live there for a long time before she was reluctantly rehoused.

At the bus station Gran would put me on the front seat of the double-decker, pay the conductor and tell him where to put me off. Parents would be quite happy to trust a ten-year-old child to make this two mile journey alone late at night. It would no longer be wise, of course, but in the 1950s children were able to enjoy a far greater amount of freedom.

SUNDAY BEST

S UNDAYS were held sacred in the 1950s. Strictly, there were no garden
bonfires, it was a disgrace to be seen hanging out washing and car mainte-
nance in the avenue was frowned upon. Noisy workmen would be told quite
firmly to STOP! Most folk – saints and sinners alike – were dedicated to keeping Sunday special.

As children we were discouraged from playing in the street, forbidden to
watch television and certainly never allowed to shop . . . and ours was not a
particularly religious household. A squabble over the roast dinner was the
only disturbance which might interrupt our peaceful little household.

Around mid-morning Father would be sharpening the carving knife on the
back doorstep while Mother was tying up the fatty joint with string and the
honey-toned presenters of *Two Way Family Favourites* (Bill Crozier and Jean
McDonald) were reuniting loved ones serving in forces around the world on
our crackly radio as I frantically searched for my collection money.
Condensation was already streaming from the kitchen windows as I prised
open the sticky front door and stepped into Carter Avenue.

Twice on Sunday I was parceled off wearing my Sunday best suit (grey jack-
et with short trousers, white shirt and fiercely knotted tie), hair Brylcreamed
with a side parting and a Bible tucked under my arm to Sunday School. I had
a certain smug smile as I walked across the fields to the village; this disappeared only when I passed my mates playing football on the scrubland behind

the prefabs. Barry Dutton needed me for goalie but Jesus wanted me for a sunbeam . . .

Mongeham Baptist Chapel had been built at the turn of the century by labourers who worked voluntarily, and even donated materials – everything from cement to hot water pipes. Today it stands between two pubs in the centre of the village, a modest brick building with a memorial stone embedded above the doorway bearing testimony to the devotion of the labourers: 'Let us rise up and build.'

The chapel emphasised the social distinction of the villagers for, while the poorer children crowded into Sunday School, the offspring of richer folk attended matins with their parents at Saint Martin's Church. Looking down on us. High on the hill.

Mongeham Chapel was warm and friendly. Inside, our rectangular schoolroom was lined with matchboard. The plastered green walls were decorated with illuminated texts which we found impossible to decipher. There were opaque arched windows, a rostrum for the speaker, a pipe organ in one corner and white china lamps which hung on chains – hovering like angels – around the tall ceiling.

The congregation sat on hard wooden forms. Alternate rows had swing backs so that they could accommodate classes, but these were later replaced by tip-up bucket seats from the redundant Regent Cinema. A curious mixture of religious and secular!

Our leader, Mr Harmer, was a melancholy gentleman. Invariably, he dressed in a dark brown suit with a gold watchchain and a trilby hat. He cycled over from his drab lodgings in Deal each week, purposely removing his cycle clips before unlocking the stout door of the chapel to give access to the rowdy village children. He could rarely keep order and sometimes suffered appalling rudeness but he was prepared to do this in order to add a spiritual dimension to our lives. He was, himself, a 'rescued drinker' and a staunch member of the Rechabites. I have much to be thankful to him for.

On weekdays Mr Harmer ran what was optimistically called a general store. He never seemed to have anything to sell. His only customers were flies and wasps. Inside there was a dark mahogany counter with jars of sticky sweets. Outside there was a rickety stall displaying half empty boxes of fruit and vegetables. On sunny days he dozed, his hat over his face, in a deckchair on the pavement dreaming of his reward in Heaven.

Every week Mr Harmer falteringly related a story, invariably with a moral, culled from Edwardian children's books. There was the Welsh history, *Mary Jones' Bible,* and the sentimental novel, *Teddy's Button.* My favourite was the imaginative fable: *The House with The Golden Windows.* 'A young girl who was dissatisfied with her life often looked with envy at a house across the valley. It appeared to belong to a prosperous family because even its windows were made of gold. One morning she decided to get up early and travel all day until she could trace the source of such wealth. When she arrived she came across a tumbledown cottage with a crippled girl leaning on the garden gate staring into the far distance. She explained her errand and her disappointment at not finding the home of her dreams. "But there it is, over there!" cried the crippled child. "I stare at it longingly every summer evening." And she pointed at the traveller's own cottage aglow in the setting sun. Now her own house had golden windows.'

Each week we were given tracts as a reward for our attentiveness or good behaviour. These consisted of colourful illustrations of vintage motor cars, historic aeroplanes, wild animals or rare flowers accompanied by a Biblical text. We collected them like cigarette cards for swaps after the service.

Our Sunday School Superintendent was a retired builder, Harry Powell, a stocky gentleman with a shock of white hair and a ruddy face that could, on occasions, swell with pomposity. Fortnightly, he would relate episodes from *Pilgrim's Progress,* with its striking imagery: the boy so bound up in his own misery that he didn't see the crown held over his head; the boatman who looked one way as he rowed in the opposite direction and the man who cheated on his path through life by jumping over the wall . . .

At other times it was *The Old Testament* when his tales took on epic proportions. As he strutted about the tiny rostrum miming the stances and gestures of each character we held our breath and watched in awe as David slew Goliath with his sling, Daniel braved the lions' den or the walls of Jericho came tumbling down. Then, at the most exciting moment, he would say: '. . . we'll see what happens next week!' and a huge groan went up from the children. Just like Saturday morning cinema! I had been privileged to hear the last in the tradition of great Victorian storytellers.

Guest speakers occasionally appeared, and the most welcome was a certain Mr Best from the neighbouring village of Adisham. He was a soft-spoken, middle-aged man with a kindly face and pure white hair. He had the enviable technique of holding the attention of noisy children by simply bringing a host of objects to show as he talked. Themes, for instance, might be lamps ('I am the light of the world.' John 8 v 12) or washing powders ('Though your sins be as scarlet they shall be white as snow.' Isaiah 1 v 18). His striking style of teaching was definitely influenced by the modern form of advertisement on television.

One evening each month in winter there was a magic lantern show. The entire village crowded into the schoolroom and sat in darkness on the hard wooden forms to stare at a clean white sheet suspended from the ceiling. Mr Harmer stooped to read the story from a notebook by the faint light from his japanned tin lantern as the painted pictures paraded magically on to our improvised silver screen.

We were held in rapture. Hazy images appeared, revealing visions of past times, remote worlds and animal kingdoms. Kids' cruelty, though, was often displayed because we howled with derision when a slide was shown upside down, or melted when it pressed against the hot lens.

Sets of slides were hired from a firm in London but the stories they told were unfamiliar and quite unsuitable for children mainly impressing upon us the temptations and miseries which lay ahead in adult life. There was a particularly vivid slide of a publican pouring his barrels down the drain. Yet in the days before colour television, and when children's books were printed in monochrome, those magic lantern shows were the highlight of my childhood.

Every so often it was announced that this was Temperance Sunday. A visiting speaker warned us fervently against the evils of strong drink and we solemnly promised that we would Stand Firm whenever temptation came our way. Above the piano was a painted scroll with room for one hundred converts and children were encouraged at an early age 'to sign the pledge'. Shamefully, I confess, I broke my promise at the age of twelve, lured by a stolen liqueur chocolate that very Christmas . . .

To keep us on the right track a framed picture hung on the back wall illustrating The Broad and Narrow Way Through Life. This was a famous Victorian print which occasionally turns up in junk shops today. The slender, tortuous route led eventually to Heaven but, to us, the broad path seemed good for the ride. There was a tavern, a lottery, a gaming house, a pawnbroker's, discreet whoring and Sunday trains which transported passengers express to Hell.

An even more tortuous passage lead round the side of the chapel and to the back where the privies were. Their warped planked doors were difficult to open or shut. The wooden seats were splintered and the slop buckets overfull so that the stench was terrible. A zigzag design was cut into the top of the doors for ventilation. Naughty kids climbed up to look over. They were definitely not destined for Heaven,

Business finished, there was the smart dash back to the front door past the stinging nettles. Generally we were painfully stung. But Gran had the remedy. She rubbed a dock leaf into the wound until the pain subsided and wiped away tears with her embroidered handkerchief.

Music for the Sunday School came from a portable harmonium. Mrs Powell and Old Mr Phillips took turns to coax tunes out of this ancient instrument. It wheezed and moaned as they swelled air into it by trundling the twin, carpeted pedals. They trod, I think, the equivalent of a mile during the course of a service!

Hymns were printed on large sheets let down from the ceiling but mainly we sang just the choruses learned from memory. Choruses formed the main part of our worship and were an important communal activity. On reflection the words were rather trite: 'Climb, Climb Up Sunshine Mountain', 'I am H-A-P-P-Y', 'Give Me Oil in My Lamp, Keep Me Burning' . . . and one which ended 'You in your small corner, and I in mine.' We were often encouraged to compete in the singing, boys against the girls, or combine to 'raise the roof'. Our primitive efforts must have alarmed many a passer-by. The best choruses involved actions: 'Wide, wide as the ocean . . . (arms outstretched), High as the heavens above . . . (reaching upwards), Deep, deep as the deepest sea (hands touching the floor) Is my Saviour's love (hands across the breast).

A visiting missionary recently returned from Africa once taught us to sing 'I will make you Fishers of Men' in Congolese. We chanted the nonsensical sounds ('Ebo, Debo, Elas, Awa . . .') through several verses, proud of our achievement. Much later I heard another Sunday School sing the strange foreign version so I wonder how far this fervent preacher travelled rural Kent?

At evening services Percy Phillips played the large pipe organ. This was a grand instrument made by the celebrated Browne's Organ Works originally based at Deal. Air needed to be pumped into it from behind and for this purpose a young assistant used to disappear behind the curtain as soon as a hymn was announced. For his weekly exertions he received the princely sum of sixpence.

Percy Phillips' arthritic hands raced across the keyboards and his feet danced over the wooden pedals which created musical effects including tremendous swells. He had been the organist since the chapel first opened and when he retired in his late seventies he movingly played 'God be with you till we meet again' as the congregation departed.

Halfway through the service the collection plate was passed around while we sang this chorus ad infinitum:

Hear the pennies dropping.
Listen while they fall.
Everyone for Jesus.
He shall have them all.

Who got the sixpences and shillings remains a mystery but certainly Jesus had all our pennies – bright shiny copper coins – as they dropped reluctantly from each tightly clenched fist into the round wooden plates.

Occasionally there were competitions – painting a text, reciting verses from scripture or cramming as many items as possible into a Swan Vestas matchbox. One challenge was to collect the largest number of 'bun' pennies in a certain period of time. Bun pennies referred to the obverse of the coin which showed the profile of Queen Victoria wearing her hair in the style known as a bun. Gran, who was a Sunday School teacher, used to wind her long hair into a bun each night before retiring to bed.

Grandma Jones spent many hours preparing her Sunday School lesson. She copied it out in careful copperplate handwriting on to loose paper which she then placed between the wafer thin India paper sheets of her Bible. Gran's Bible was the most precious item in her house and nothing was ever allowed

to be placed on top of it. She used it as a file for all her personal correspondence and anything important which she wanted 'to trust to the Lord'. When she died, it was found to contain an assortment of religious tracts, toffee wrappers, newspaper cuttings, Patience Strong poems, pressed flowers, crumpled photographs, obituaries and treasured last letters from members of her family.

In later years she travelled to Sunday School in a young teacher's combination motorcycle/sidecar. Gran would exchange her woollen beret for a helmet, squeeze into the bullet shaped sidecar and be whisked off at an alarming speed the short distance to Mongeham. It was a strange experience to see this frail Edwardian lady travel by combo to chapel clutching her Bible. Nothing would prevent her from fulfilling her Christian ministry.

Mid July there was the summer treat. It was broadcast long in advance that there would be an excursion to a neighbouring resort – alternately Folkestone or Broadstairs. Today it seems inconceivable the excitement this announcement generated. Suddenly our schoolroom was packed every Sunday with children eager to obtain the six weekly 'stars' stamped on their attendance card which would entitle them to attend The Outing.

Three battered coaches arrived at the Sunday School early one weekday morning and there was a mad scramble aboard by the village children accompanied by their mums and a few dads most of whom I, as a regular attender, didn't know. A short journey . . . a dash for the beach . . . deckchairs . . . hampers . . . beach umbrellas . . . suntan oil . . . shrimping nets . . . bathing costumes . . . box cameras . . . buckets and spades . . . and a rush into the sea!

Broadstairs Bay was ringed by seaweed which tough kids raced through into deep water where they swam and dived and splashed and played with carefree aban-

don. I, as a non-swimmer, was left alone to paddle at the water's edge. To break the monotony I built sandcastles in the circle of deckchairs occupied by parents until it was time to munch the homemade rhubarb and ginger jam sandwiches – now filled with sand and attacked by wasps – packed by mum for my solitary picnic.

At teatime we retreated to a host chapel where kindly pinafored helpers waited on us with half huffkins, iced buns and weak tea. Cricket followed on a nearby green (one had to be athletic to appreciate Sunday School treats) before it was time to return. Tired, we sank into the deep leather seats for a roundabout coach ride and community singing (hymns at the front/pop songs at the rear) until we reached home where, as a final treat, we received a brown paper bag with an apple and an orange.

In late summer we held a Children's Flower Festival. These were not the grand thematic affairs of the modern Anglican Church. Simplicity was the keynote and we were encouraged to scour the countryside and woodlands for wild flowers to bring rather than cuttings from our gardens. Our modest bunches were placed in borrowed cut glass or enamel vases on a trestle table laid with a pure white cloth. We were encouraged to tie a text from the Bible on each bunch of flowers which were later distributed to elderly folk in the village.

In September there was Harvest Festival. A table was placed before the rostrum laden with home-grown produce, and in the days immediately after the

91

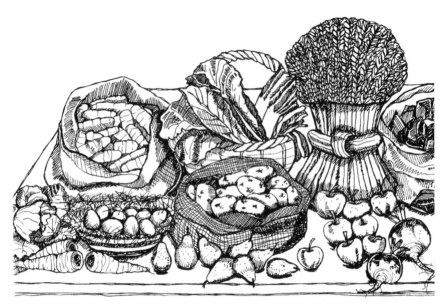

war when fruit and vegetables were scarce, here was a bumper feast! There were some truly imaginative ideas – a net with fish caught fresh from the sea, free range eggs and, one inspired touch, a sack of coal as a reminder of the three thriving local mines, Betteshanger, Tilmanstone and Snowdon. For the centrepiece our village baker had baked an enormous loaf in the shape of a wheatsheaf (remember when corn stood in stooks or sheaves?). I was regarded as a real 'townie', turning up with my tin of carrots from the pantry in our pre-fab, and felt my humble gift spurned. God grew the vegetables but Satan owned the canning factories.

Christmas was heralded by the Toy Service. Here we were encouraged to bring not our second best toy but our *best* toy to give to the local orphanage. Conscience-stricken, I solemnly parceled up my recent birthday gift of a Hornby Dublo electric train set to take to the chapel on the following Sunday. Once my intention was discovered there was a lot of to-ing and fro-ing between my parents and the Superintendent. I was mystified, when my mother helped me unwrap the train set and replace it with a third rate battered tin bus.

At the end of the year there was Prize Giving. Proud parents were invited to a special service when the Superintendent presented each scholar with a crisp new book as a reward for their attendance. Inevitably it was a book concerning the exploits of missionaries. Missionaries!

One year I ventured to exchange my prize at The Christian Bookshop where I was escorted into the back room and shown the 2/6d shelves reserved for

Sunday School prizes. Even more missionaries . . . Children who skipped Sunday School to work weekends could no doubt afford the treasured Biggles, Jennings, Dr Dolittle and Billy Bunter adventures.

Occasionally I accompanied Gran to Evening Service. A marked contrast here was the air of quiet reverence as one entered the chapel. The old ladies of the village in their knitted hats warbled the descant to the accompaniment of the thunderous pipe organ. Then a great silence descended throughout the lengthy sermon which, as nonconformists, we were careful to call an 'address'.

I felt secure as I snuggled up to Gran in her worn camel coat and watched the dying sunset blaze through the high gothic windows as we sang: 'The day Thou gavest, Lord, is ended . . .' A touch of Heaven.

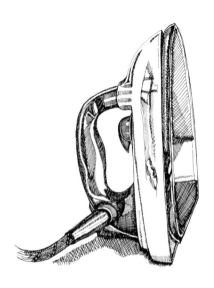

HOUSEHOLD CHORES

O N MONDAY mornings Dad would be up early getting ready for work, getting his own breakfast, getting the newspapers . . . He would attack the fire, whose dying embers the night before had left a pile of soot in the ash-pan which he emptied noisily into the dustbin. Then he would vigorously rake the fireplace, sweep the hearth and give one final rattle with the poker which announced to Mum and me that it was Time To Get Up.

Breakfast on weekdays was a hurried occasion and might consist merely of a bowl of cereal which for me had selfish motives. Kellogg's Cornflakes had wonderful free gifts concealed deep inside: miniature submarines which could be filled with baking soda so that they submerged and resurfaced in the wash-ing up bowl; cardboard whizzers which, when threaded with elastic, spun round rapidly to reveal dazzling psychedelic colours; red plastic Guards bandsmen playing cymbals, drums, trumpets and trombones as they marched in proud procession across our kitchen table.

Shredded Wheat offered press-out cardboard rocket planes and launchers while Sugar Puffs gave miniature plastic cars – Austin Healey, Morris Minor and Riley 2.6 litre. Ricicles, sugar coated rice, were promoted as being 'twici-cles as nicicles'. A toy theatre was printed on the back of Ricicles packets and when assembled it showed a scene featuring Noddy from Toyland. All my favourite characters – Mr Plod, Sly the Goblin, Tubby Bear and Bumpy Dog –

appeared as colourful cardboard cutouts. Novelty masks and puzzles printed on the reverse of cereal packets were further excuses for munching through the contents. Just occasionally the offers appealed to adults – initialled stainless steel cutlery (which my parents snapped up) and a competition to win a Dream Home or the cash equivalent (£500).

Robertson's strawberry jam was my favourite flavour. Invariably the soggy sweet fruit rose to the top of the jar. Once that was eaten I lost interest in the rest of the contents. Hidden under the lid, though, was a paper gollywog, ten of which could be exchanged through the post for an enamel badge, now collectors' items. Even Brooke Bond PG Tips tea packets offered a bribe, for there was a series of cards to collect on topics as diverse as Butterflies of the World, The Saga of Ships, Trees In Britain and The Race Into Space to stick in informative booklets. (The first album was British Birds in 1954 with a commentary by Tunnicliffe).

We had tasteful pale green breakfast china, an electro-plated toast rack and an assortment of Pyrex oven-to-table glass bowls. Knives and forks were laid to the side of a raffia place mat and a dessert spoon and fork primly crossed above in what we imagined to be the style of gentry. Later we learned with dismay that King George VI dismissed this fad as 'cafe culture'.

In reserve we had a set of fish knives and forks – a wedding gift – kept separately in a wooden box lined with purple velvet. Proudest possession was a set of square fish plates decorated with transfer prints of freshwater fish. Possibly these were another wedding present dating from the 1940s for they were considered too valuable to be used. Instead they were permanently displayed on our Welsh dresser. After we had dined mother used a plastic crumb tray and curved brush to sweep the gingham tablecloth; I considered this a great affectation in a prefab.

Tupperware made its appearance at the end of the decade. It began as a craze which escalated into a status symbol. To begin with it was simply a series of airtight plastic containers for the kitchen but a whole range of apparatus was added – lemon squeezers, butter dishes, egg cups, lolly moulds. We had a condiment set shaped like a space ship but the design was flawed because when you lifted out the precariously balanced salt or pepper the whole structure collapsed. Tupperware agents arranged parties for housewives in their own homes, so that they could sample the latest products. Mother's ambition was to own every single article so then she could Live Like The Queen.

Time for work. 'You wash and I'll dry.' At least we had the benefit of running hot water in our prefab which meant that washing up dirty dishes was almost a pleasure. That done, Mother would don her trews, roll up her sleeves and tie a headscarf into a turban in the manner of a wartime factory worker before hunting for mops and brooms, feather dusters and household cleansers. I volunteered to help with simple chores since these would earn points towards my pocket money.

One task was laying the fire. First yesterday's newspaper was torn in strips and scrunched up into balls. These musn't be too tight otherwise the air would be trapped and the fire would not catch. Paper formed the bottom layer in the open grate. Father would already have chopped a supply of thin wooden sticks which were laid criss-cross over the newspaper to form a second layer. Finally, small lumps of coal were placed on top.

The fire was lit by a match from the bottom – the newspaper ignited the sticks which burned fast and set fire to the coal. Lastly, you carefully added the large lumps of coal with tongs once a steadily smoking fire was ensured. In the Fifties a copper coal scuttle or brass log box, and a swivelling companion set consisting of brush, poker, dustpan and tongs, were general accompaniments to the hearth.

There were tricks of the trade to start a lax fire. Sprinkling sugar on top usually did the trick but a double page of newspaper held across the fireplace allowing the air to 'draw' from underneath was an alternative ruse. When you least expected it, though, the paper caught alight and had to be hastily extinguished.

Most homes had a mirror above the fireplace. My parents considered this dangerous so instead they displayed a framed lush chocolate box picture of swans sailing on a river, by Vernon Ward. Mother did have a curious habit of lifting up her skirt to warm her bottom by the fire on cold mornings. This was the first time I glimpsed the full regalia of women's underwear complete with petticoat, stocking tops and suspenders.

A brass toasting fork hung by our fireside. It was assumed that it would keep a child amused to make his own toast at tea times. Indeed the first slice was a novelty although you generally singed your fingers turning the bread over. And after the second slice your arm began to wilt and the whole task became a burden once the novelty wore off.

Open fires, though, had a pure joy which today's children may never experience. Toasting chestnuts by the fire in winter time was wonderful. They hissed and crackled and blackened on the grate. Once their shells split they were considered ready for eating. Generally I ate far more than my share thus ensuring violent tummy ache all night.

Alternatively, you could sit staring into the fire, making pictures of the blue and orange flames while listening to the wireless. A sudden gust of wind rushing down the chimney would denote an unwelcome change in the weather. At times Mother would point to a streak of soot dangling from the grate and announce: 'There's a stranger on the bar'. Traditionally, this meant we would soon have a visitor and sometimes there was truth in our strange family superstition.

Another superstition involved the eight day chiming clock which stood on the mantelpiece. This was another wedding gift from Dad's mother in Derby. One morning we awoke to find that it had stopped in the early hours and nothing would induce it to restart. This was an omen, warned Mother, and she insisted that bad news was to follow. Sure enough, around noon, a despatch rider arrived on his motorcycle with a telegram from Derby. Grandma had died in the night. Dad was recalled from work and immediately went into mourning. For a whole month he wore a black tie and armbands. There was a scramble for Mum to find suitable clothes for the funeral: neighbours lent black dress, black shoes, black hat . . . Three days later Mother and Father went by train to the funeral, leaving me in the care of Gran.

Telegrams kept people in touch with urgent news before the wide availability of telephones. They arrived in tiny orange envelopes and their message was printed in capital letters by ticker tape stuck on a half sheet of cheap paper. There was only one prefab on our estate in which a telephone had been installed. The woman stood in the window to make her calls and thereby ensured that her high status was admired by all the neighbours. She did, however, share a party line which meant that she often had to wait for her unseen partner to finish a call before lifting the receiver.

In the 1950s local calls could be dialled direct but for calls outside a twenty-five miles radius you had to go through the operator. Father never could afford for us to go 'on the blower' and so in the event of an emergency we had to seek out a public kiosk. They were complicated to operate (Press button A/Press button B). You often lost your money.

A cheaper method of keeping in touch with relatives was via the radio. We regularly requested records to be played for distant members of our family on their birthdays or anniversaries on daytime radio programmes. *Workers' Playtime* was generally broadcast from some Midlands factory but its out-moded presentation was a throwback to the last war. *Housewives' Choice* was the most popular morning show, and lively weekly guest presenters included Cliff Michelmore, Charlie Chester, Sam Costa and Pete Murray. Its mixture of warmth, humour and popular tunes certainly cheered the day while engaged in household chores.

Hoovering, though, was not conducive to the appreciation of good music.

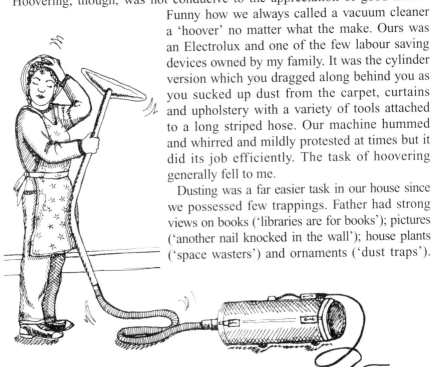

Funny how we always called a vacuum cleaner a 'hoover' no matter what the make. Ours was an Electrolux and one of the few labour saving devices owned by my family. It was the cylinder version which you dragged along behind you as you sucked up dust from the carpet, curtains and upholstery with a variety of tools attached to a long striped hose. Our machine hummed and whirred and mildly protested at times but it did its job efficiently. The task of hoovering generally fell to me.

Dusting was a far easier task in our house since we possessed few trappings. Father had strong views on books ('libraries are for books'); pictures ('another nail knocked in the wall'); house plants ('space wasters') and ornaments ('dust traps').

Wedding presents, naturally, were the source of almost all our ornaments – Carltonware soup mugs with decorative covers, an electroplate sweetmeat dish, a Crown Derby coffee set with a delicate floral pattern and a Doulton Toby jug depicting the hideous, grinning, warted John Barleycorn.

Father would have lined up the family's shoes for me to clean. We considered ourselves very poor if we didn't each have two pairs of shoes – one black, one brown – plus carpet slippers. Best shoes were kept in shape by the insertion of shaped wooden trees. A box held shoe polish, brushes and cloths. First you applied an even layer of Cherry Blossom or Kiwi shoe polish with a thick brush. Then you used a lighter brush to buff up the leather before finishing with a top shine from a yellow duster. Shoes were considered to be clean only when you could see your reflection in the surface.

Making beds was a real bore. Our beds were stripped each week ready for the wash and re-made with crisp new cotton sheets. First a bottom sheet was smoothed down, the corners neatly tucked in, before the top sheet was applied. Several layers of warm woollen blankets were added and the candlewick bedspread was placed on top as a finishing touch. Feather pillows gave me an allergy so mine were packed with foam. Clean pyjamas were folded under the pillow ready for that night.

An easier task was making 'a proper cup of tea'. Tea bags were not invented so a pot of fresh tea needed to be made and always served into tea cups, not mugs. There was a hunt for the whistle for the kettle which was three-quarters filled before placing on the gas stove. The teapot needed to be warmed first before the spoons of tea – one for each person and one for the pot – were added from the tin caddy. A dash of milk was added to each cup plus a lump or two of sugar. After brewing, tea was served through a strainer but there were generally a few specks of tea leaves floating on the surface of the cups.

Mother mopped the kitchen floor with Flash, and scoured the bathroom fittings with Vim. Our compact suite – bath, sink and loo – was in pastel green and the towelling curtains were an abstract pattern. Dad cut out pin-ups of Jayne Mansfield and Marilyn Monroe from the newspaper to stick around the toilet. There were strips of torn newspaper threaded through string when Mother couldn't afford to buy loo rolls. Deodorants and cosmetics were kept to a minimum but there was always a tin of Gibbs Dentifrice toothpaste in the form of a round pink minty flavoured tablet; a silver metal box of Cutex for Mum to polish her nails; a bar of Camay, Lux or Imperial Leather soap and a tiny bottle of Drene shampoo whenever a family hairwash was threatened.

A mirrored cabinet discreetly concealed medicinal powders and pills. Shelves were stocked with Andrews Liver Salts, a bottle of iodine, a jar of Vaseline and a roll of Elastoplast. Beechams Powders were a standby for colds and 'flu while Carter's Lttle Liver Pills regularly opened our bowels.

Baths were limited to one a week. Even so the level of the lukewarm water never rose much beyond the wartime prescription of five inches, for this was another of Father's stringent economies. Nonetheless our prefab bathroom was the envy of the village children who still bathed in a tin tub before the fire then shivered up the garden path to their privy.

Spring cleaning was a far more thorough affair. The heavy velvet winter curtains – plum or bottle green – were exchanged for a lighter floral summer pattern. The mottled glass shade from the centre light in the lounge was taken down and washed. All year round we had pretended not to notice the shadows cast by dead flies. Mats were taken up and draped over the washing line for Mother to attack with a wicker carpet beater. Sweat poured from her brow but at least she improved her style of badminton.

Monday mornings – whatever the season – were equated with 'washday

100

blues'. No self-respecting housewife would think of beginning the week without a line full of immaculate clothes billowing in the breeze. Hanging out the washing was usually the excuse for neighbours to gossip over the fence.

The gas copper in the kitchen would be lit and Mum would cram the week's washing in with wooden tongs. She was careful to separate whites from coloureds which couldn't be boiled. A rich soapy lather would be created by sprinkling powder detergent from a box of Fairy Snow, Tide or Dreft. At intervals mother would pummel the clothes with a copper posser, just like Gran. Special items like Dad's shirts would be dealt with separately. Collars and cuffs of my school shirts were scrubbed with a stiff brush and Lifebuoy soap on a glass ribbed washboard by hand in the sink. Rub–a–dub–dub.

There were no rubber gloves so Mum's hands were often chafed and sore. Soap tended to turn whites yellow so for the final rinse a Reckitt's Blue bag was swished around in the water. This was a little linen bag filled with a fine powder which ensured that the shirts came up pure white. Items were then folded and passed through a wringer to squeeze out excess water. When not in use our wringer folded neatly into a small table with a servicable enamel top. Lastly clothes were carried in a plastic basket into the back garden where they were hung with wooden pegs on the line stretched between two concrete posts and propped up with a rustic Y-shaped pole.

When Mother earned more money as a teacher she was able to afford to hire one of the new-fangled twin tubs (combined washing machine and spin dryer). These were delivered to the house by van for her to use for a few hours. Later still, when coin–operated launderettes opened up, Mum left our clothes for a service wash while shopping. All the same she had to cycle with it, there and back, a full two miles into the town.

Ironing followed soon afterwards. Mother wisely invested in a sturdy Morphy Richards electric iron. But there was an absence of wall sockets in our prefab so mum also bought an adaptor which she screwed into the light bulb socket. It meant she had to stand in the centre of the room with the flex trailing from the ceiling as she ironed. Everything was ironed – tea towels, string vests, napkins, handkerchiefs, pyjamas, runners, dusters – a monumental task. Mother stood with headscarf and cigarette still listening to the radio pressing an eternity of Dad's work shirts. Their collars would have been sent separately to the laundry to be starched. Even the invention of nylon drip-dry shirts offered little relief for Father insisted that these, too, were pressed. They were buttoned and folded and as a final touch plastic stiffeners were slipped into the corners of the collars.

It was traditional to break for elevenses. Invariably, a neighbour would call round for a quick cup of coffee. Generally, this was Camp coffee, a thick brown syrup contained in a slim bottle with a label showing an Indian servant serving a tray of steaming beverage to a Scots Guard. Nescafé and Maxwell House instant coffee became available but we hadn't yet acquired the taste for it. Often the Camp coffee was mixed with a spoonful of Carnation, sickly sweet evaporated milk. Mother was a secret smoker so she would send me to the corner shop to buy five Guards or Park Drive tipped cigarettes. Workmen smoked Player's Weights, Senior Service, Woodbines or Will's Whiffs. Cigarettes might be bought singly at that time, stored in a glass jar and wrapped in a paper bag like sweets.

Most things were still delivered to the door in the 1950s. Lorries with open trailers brought coal from the local collieries to the avenue. We felt sorry for the men with their blackened faces and bent backs as they cheerfully carried the sacks round to our coalshed. The dustcart came in the middle of the week. Menfolk struggled to line up the hefty bins on the pavement ready for collection by a small lorry. It had a large semi–circular container with curved sliding doors to conceal the rubbish. Milk came on silent electrically-operated floats in the early morning, and the chink of the bottles as they were dumped on the doorstep was a signal to wake up for school.

An ice cream van optimistically drove up the avenue playing inane chimes every Sunday afternoon and a Walls vanilla briquette was an occasional

102

teatime treat. Mobile shops became popular for a time. They were presumed to be handy for shoppers who had to travel miles into town. Housewives considered the prices of the meat van exorbitant, however, so this novel idea was of brief duration. Vegetables arrived on a wooden cart pulled by a sturdy farmhorse owned by Mr Carter. It was heavily laden but the choice of fruit and vegetables was limited. Everything came in season. Canned foods always tasted tinny. Frozen foods were in their infancy. In any case we grew our own vegetables since a sizeable allotment was attached to our prefab. It was often my job to peel homegrown vegetables – more pocket money – and I have a fond memory of sitting on the back doorstep shelling peas into a colander under the shade of our mauve lilac tree.

Monday was the traditional day for eating leftovers from the Sunday joint – cold meat and pickles with bubble and squeak. Dad might eat – alone – a pig's trotter with mustard. The bottle of HP sauce never failed to materialise and I studied the label to learn my first French: '*La sauce HP est un melange de haute qualite de fruits orientaux, d'epices et de vinaigre . . .*' Father might join us for lunch (as a working class family we called our midday meal dinner) but on other weekdays he would expect the regulation meat and two veg.

On rare occasions meat was carved at the table. Poultry was a great luxury and might appear only once or twice a year but it was farm fresh not frozen and so tasted delicious. Mother always dished vegetables straight out of the pans and onto our plates. Piping hot!

Typical postwar meals were shepherd's pie, Lancashire hotpot, liver and bacon, tripe and onions, sausage and mash, steak and kidney pie or pudding. When we were hard up there might be rabbit stew, fish pie, macaroni cheese

103

or the dreaded corned beef hash. Greens were obligatory but these were over-cooked until they were tasteless. Heavy meals rather than healthy ones seemed the rule of the day. Economic rather than edible. And there were few concessions to children. 'Take it or leave it' was the cook's maxim.

Lunch was limited to two courses. If tinned soup were served it signalled no dessert. Sweets were equally unimaginative and there was never an alternative of fruit or cheese. Milk puddings were the easy option – tapioca, semolina, sago or rice with a dot of jam in the centre. Rolypoly pudding, spotted dick, rhubarb crumble, bread and butter pudding, baked apples or banana and custard were served when Mother was feeling adventurous. Family favourites were blackberry, gooseberry or redcurrant pies and the mouthwatering queen's pudding. Stewed prunes were made bearable by counting the number of stones left on the side of the bowl: 'Tinker, tailor, soldier, sailor . . .'

Mum excelled at teas, especially on Sundays. Tinned salmon was served in sandwiches cut diagonally with the crusts removed. A simple salad – lettuce, tomatoes and cucumber – accompanied them. There would be slices of beetroot soaking in vinegar and spring onions dipped in salt. Afterwards there was ice cream and fruit jelly (blackcurrant, greengage, tangerine) served in shallow green sundae dishes. Sometimes there was also a lemon meringue pie, a blancmange which tasted like soft soap or a sherry trifle sprinkled with hundreds and thousands whose colours ran all over the topping. For a real treat mum might have bought me some alphabet biscuits or iced diamonds. At the centre of the table there would be a little china horseshoe-shaped posy bowl filled, perhaps, with pansies, nasturtiums or forget-me-nots, which were Mother's favourite flower.

Mum might attempt some baking – jam tarts, coconut madelaines, cream horns or butterfly cakes. When she had finished I might be allowed to taste the cake mix by licking my finger after running it round the rim of the large pottery bowl. It was fun, too, when cakes were served on edible rice paper. Favourites were iced buns coloured pink with cochineal and decorated with glacé cherries, candied angelica and tooth breaking silver balls. There might be a victoria sponge made from a Mary Baker's or Green's cake mix, or a bought Battenberg. A fresh pot of tea was placed on the table and poured into fine bone china cups through a silver strainer.

Meals were always eaten at the kitchen table and were a family occasion. All the same they were conducted in strict silence which was considered the height of good manners and any idle childish chatter was punished. After finishing my meal I was made to wait until Father had finished his last mouthful before asking to be excused from the table.

On Thursdays it was half-day closing for all the shops in the town. Father cycled home promptly at one o 'clock for lunch which would be waiting to be served straight on to the table. Free afternoons were not an opportunity for recreational visits or family outings but a time of general inspection of the morning's housework. Cleanliness was not next to godliness in our household, it quite surpassed religion. Dust and dirt brought pangs of guilt. Neglected tasks ensured a bout of conscience. There was no chance for Mother to laze in the sunshine – the drone of Father's hoover going over missed bits or the clatter of tools being Put Away Properly discarded peace. Far easier to get up and start all over again . . .

PRIMARY COLOURS

R UTH ELLIS was taken from her cell and hanged this morning at nine o'clock . . .' the BBC newsreader announced in his clipped tones immediately after Big Ben had ominously boomed nine times. This alarming information was relayed over the radio on the wall of our classroom where we sat in silence – hymn books open at the ready – while our teacher marked the register. Promptly at five past nine each Tuesday morning we joined in the BBC religious broadcast to schools – hymns, prayers, stories and meditations. And in this incidental manner we learned the fate of convicted murderers Derek Bentley, Timothy Evans and John Christie before corporately praising God for his infinite mercies . . .

Mongeham School was opened in 1950. A sprawling complex, it was a single-storeyed building shaped in the letter E. Future historians may deduce this was in deference to the dawning age of the new Elizabethans. The entire middle wing was devoted to infants, the top wing to juniors. Classrooms were light and spacious with doors leading on to patios for open-air lessons in summer. The facilities included a sports field, a fan-shaped hall, a dining room and a grand foyer with a mural depicting Kentish smugglers. Fifty years later it still serves the needs of modern pupils and is ably equipped for teaching the National Curriculum.

My first day at school was some time in the autumn of 1953. In those days pupils were entitled to attend immediately after their fifth birthday. This meant that I joined classmates who already knew the ropes and who were reluctant to admit a stranger into their midst. All the same it was not a full class since several children had taken time off to go hop picking.

For weeks Mum had been sewing Cash's name tapes into every item of school clothing and painstakingly printing my name in indelible ink into the side of my plimsolls or pumps. Dad bought me a shiny new leather satchel whose pockets soon bulged with such educational requirements as catapults, conkers and slings. My pockets brimmed with other schoolboy essentials – magnet, compass, penknife, marbles and Beechnut chewing gum.

Finally the Great Day came. Mother left me at the school gates – no tears here for I was looking forward to the adventure – and I joined the straggly line of older pupils snatching girls' ribbons and slinging boys' caps over the hedges. Eventually a smiling teacher led me into the spacious modern classroom. As a treat I was allowed to choose a toy from the activity box to play with while she called the register.

My eyes alighted on a little wooden stand pierced with assorted holes, a selection of shapes and a gaily coloured rubber mallet. Bliss!

'Adams?' BANG 'Brown?' BANG! 'Carter?' BANG! 'Dutton?' BANG! BANG! BANG! Suddenly, the young teacher sprinted across her classroom, snatched my mallet midair and – minus that smile – purposely placed it on the desk. How easily pupil's reputations are made . . .

Most mornings after that began with a whole school assembly. The headmistress, Miss Nicholls, stood on a rostrum and conducted a short religious service in her strict, formal manner. There was a hymn and a prayer followed by notices and moans. Hymns, though, seemed a marvellous way to start the day. 'Morning has broken, like the first morning . . .' was my favourite for it

107

smacked of the countryside with its promise of a fresh start to each new day.
'Blackbird has spoken, like the first bird . . .'

Frequently hymns had a maritime flavour. Living in a seaside town, 'Eternal
Father, strong to save . . .' had a poignancy on stormy mornings when Walmer
lifeboat was launched to assist in coastal rescues. 'When lamps are lighted in
the town, the boats sail out to sea . . .' was another memorable hymn that aptly
pictured local fishermen toiling all night off shore.

At Mongeham School classes were large, in excess of forty pupils. We sat at
hard wooden desks resolutely facing the blackboard. Two-by-two. Like animals in Noah's Ark. The varnished lids incised with graffiti had grooves for
pens and wells for ink. The boys had buck teeth with braces; the girls pink
plastic National Health spectacles. Pigtails and pony tails. Greedyguts,
Copycats, Clever-dicks and Spoil-sports. Cry babies, Sneaks, Cowardy
Custards and Nosey Parkers.

School uniform was a serviceable maroon and grey – caps, ties, jumpers and
blazers. The school badge sported the county emblem – a rearing white horse.
I had gloves sewn on to string threaded through the arms of my gabardine
raincoat and long socks with elastic garters which bit into my legs and left
purple runnels round my calves. All the boys wore short trousers (a remnant
of material shortages after the war) until several years into secondary school.

Junior school classrooms, although formal were packed with interest. Walls
were decorated with colourful pictures which formed the centrefold of the teachers' publication, *Child Education*. Teachers' own visual aids were in profusion,

plus cuttings from the daily newspapers and also maps proudly proclaiming the pink bits that marked the extent of the British Empire. During my last term I recall that the entire back wall was given over to a chart plotting the movement of cruise ships from merchant shipping lines which we contacted via Lloyds List. Captains and crews from the New Zealand line, the Blue Funnel, the White Star, the Pacific and Orient replied with personal letters and generous packages for display.

For schools radio was an important teaching resource. Each weekday there were special educational broadcasts accompanied by colourful brochures which helped us to visualise crickets mating or moths pupating. Music, literature and nature were effectively taught in this manner. We listened politely if not intently. Most popular was *Music and Movement*. We spilled into the school hall in our gym gear to find a space by ourselves and 'when the music stops' become a tree, a bus or a (well behaved) monster. More robust was PE with apparatus such as bucks, vaulting horses, trampolines and medicine balls forming a mini assault course.

Discipline was tough. Perhaps it had to be with large classes. But it wasn't always fair. I was a bright child and jumped classes, which created unwelcome extra work for the harassed teacher. The deputy headmaster at one time rejoiced in the name of Mr Fright. I was an extrovert in a humourless age. Worse still I came from The Prefabs. I was a marked man. To gain attention the teacher lobbed missiles – chalk, blackboard rubbers, piles of exercise books . . .

The cane was wielded frequently although to ring the changes plimsolls, rulers, cricket bats and even rounders batons descended on boys' bottoms. Girls merely had their wrists slapped or were made to write one hundred lines. The mildest reprimand to pupils resulted in missing playtime by standing nose pressed against the blackboard or behind the door in the waste paper bin. No one dared complain to their parents for fear of receiving a double dose. A good hiding.

Once my mother turned up unannounced at the school to see the headmistress and as she passed along the corridor she saw me hauled out yet again for punishment. She flung open the classroom door and called out to my bad tempered teacher: 'You've got the wrong boy – it was that one!' And promptly slammed it shut. Even the Caped Crusader could not have had more perfect timing.

Maths = misery. Mental, Mechanical, Problems. Fractions, Equations, Theorems. For ten minutes every morning we chanted our tables. 'One two is two; two twos are four . . .' I learned to mime so although my lips moved no sound spilled forth. This was followed by forty sums scrawled on the black-

109

board to be completed without the aid of modern calculators by break time. Hundreds, tens and units; yards, feet and inches; litres, gallons and pints; pounds, shillings and pence. Decimalisation spelled an end to such torment.

We carefully practised handwriting progressing from thick pencils to dip pens. The style taught was stick and ball evolved by a certain Marion Richardson. Eventually we mastered joined up writing. No loops were permissible for fear of blotting the characters. Parents intent upon their offspring reaching grammar school presented them with a reliable Osmiroid or Parker pen.

Writing was generally accompanied by a picture, a deliberate tactic for slowing brighter pupils down. It was a great reward to colour with chump wax crayons ('remember to share. . .') while duller pupils struggled with mindless copying from the board. I still have my Scripture book showing the birth of Jesus, the call of the disciples, the feeding of the five thousand and the crucifixion with Pontius Pilate arriving post-haste by helicopter.

The emphasis of postwar education was firmly on the three Rs – Reading, wRiting and aRithmetic. But this was carefully balanced with creative subjects which generally occupied whole afternoons. Compositions were strictly marked for spellings and grammar by our class teacher who had been invalided during the war when he had been required to censor soldiers' letters home. 'Nice' and 'got' and 'Just a line to say . . .' were ruthlessly crossed out.

On Thursday afternoons throughout the seasons the upper junior boys had

compulsory gardening. Girls were engaged in weaving or embroidery, shielded from the elements. A thin ribbon of land which ran the entire length of the school was divided into neat square plots managed by teams of diffident pupils. Perhaps here, too, was a remnant of the war: Dig for Victory; Hoe for Education?

We shivered and sulked as we dodged the showers. Tedium was enlivened with bouts of throwing spades at rivals' wellies or slinging slugs at neighbours' wheelbarrows. Whenever the master patrolled we would, naturally, be engaged in tending vegetables with trowels, trugs, dibbers, sieves and rakes.

Flowers were scorned because everything had to have a Practical Purpose. Self sufficiency was hardly the motif, all the same. since the fruits of our labours were offered for sale at prices parents could rarely afford. On wet afternoons our muddy boots retreated to the classroom where we merely drew in our gardening notebooks. Admittedly the orderly rows of sketched vegetables bore little resemblance to our weedy efforts but at least I could appreciate the exercise on a purely artistic level.

Infant activities, of course, had been far more adventurous. The sand tray was a popular choice with plastic moulds in the shapes of mermaids, crabs and starfish. This was the nearest some kids ever got to the beach. Additionally there was a potter's wheel but this was rarely used as it caused such a mess. Yet arts and crafts were encouraged and miniature double-sided easels were provided for budding artists. We stood wearing fathers' old shirts daubing paper with thick brushes dipped in powder paint. Red suns, blue skies, green trees, yellow flowers. Primary colours. Houses had a central door, windows squashed into each corner and a smoky chimney . . . cats had wide eyes and long whiskers . . . mums wore floral skirts and silly smiles. Once satisfied, the background was filled in afterwards.

Is it my imagination or did we really have beds with itchy grey blankets to lie down for part of every afternoon? Certainly the majority of activities were designed to make us grow Big and Strong. School milk was delivered daily in heavy crates in third-pint bottles to be sucked through bent straws before

morning break. In winter the cream on top would turn to ice. One kindly mistress had the bright idea of letting us cultivate mustard and cress on blotting paper which she placed on sunny window ledges. Later she brought in a loaf and butter to make sandwiches for us to munch away with our free school milk. We loved her.

The Welfare State ensured that children's health was regulated. Periodically the 'nit nurse' inspected our hair class by class. We convinced ourselves that nits preferred clean heads. She towered over us with sharp cold instruments, investigating our tousled locks. She looked like she was eating a Chinese meal with

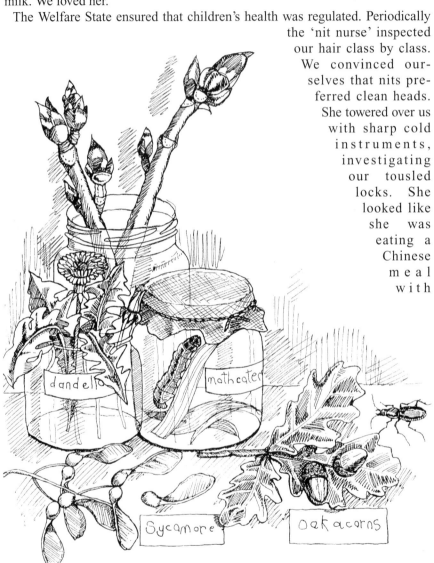

chopsticks. Nervously we bared arms to the school doctor for jabs against measles, whooping cough and polio. He weighed us and measured our heights. Mothers were invited to attend the inspection while their offspring shivered in string vests in the medical room. I still retain the moment of horror as the doctor's hands ventured down my pants.

Spasmodically, the school dentist made his visit, unannounced. He arrived in a touring caravan, so obviously he regarded this in the nature of a holiday. For us it was sheer misery. He poked and prodded in our tiny mouths behind the portable screens. We feared the dreaded drill which he operated with his foot while forcing your Mouth Open Wide. Once he dropped it on my tongue. Before the introduction of fluoride into drinking water the dentist was guaranteed to find several teeth needing attention.

At least the loss of milk teeth had a financial benefit because if you slipped one under your pillow last thing at night a fairy would replace it with a silver sixpence. Honest! Cross my heart and hope to die . . . Adult teeth were more of a problem. I had too many, apparently, which pushed my front teeth out like a rabbit. A brace was prescribed to be worn morning, noon and night. I had to go along periodically to have it tightened which resulted in ulcers and abscesses, abscesses and ulcers . . .

Generally you went to hospital for an extraction. Mum didn't tell you anything but kept you at home from school without breakfast saying you were going 'somewhere special.' While a nurse held you down, an anaesthetist placed a pad of lint into a wire sieve, dropped ether on to it from a brown ribbed bottle and clamped it tight to your face. 'There's nothing to worry about,' the nurse soothed. 'Just take deep breaths and you'll drift off to sleep.' This was a dreadful sensation, it felt like a steam roller riding over you, before you were mercifully overtaken by oblivion.

Older children might be forced to sit bolt upright in the dentist's chair while a doctor arrived to administer gas. At home you were repeatedly sick from the anaesthetic and so had to recuperate in bed all afternoon clutching a cuddly toy. Adults as well as children were required to take a friend along with them as a precaution when they were due for an extraction.

Happily, on fine days we went for nature walks holding hands in pairs in a crocodile line following the perimeter of the school field. Our finds were displayed on a little corner table which faithfully recorded the changes in the seasons. Catkins gave way to conkers; tadpoles turned into frogs. Caterpillars munched contentedly on leaves stuck into jam jars with holes pierced in their paper lids. Dead beetles were laid to rest on cotton wool stuffed into Swan Vestas matchboxes. Toadstools, lichens, fossils, feathers, acorn pipes, ash keys and sycamore helicopters were all neatly labelled. So, too, were wild flowers –

scabious, campion, dandelion, ragwort, deadnettle – picked from nearby woods and rammed into vases on our very own Class Nature Table.

Bird's nesting was a popular pastime with boys. Over weekends we would share the secrets of a blackbird's or songthrush's nest which we looted without shame to win house points for classroom display. I remember bringing in a complete spider's web which I found glistening with morning dew strung between twigs of hawthorn as I skipped to school one summer's day.

Playtime was a real social occasion. Marbles, jackstones, conkers all appeared in due season. Regular as clockwork. Children huddled in corners to cheer rival groups for these were spectator sports.

Choosing teams or partners for playtime games had its own ritual. If you wanted to be a captain you had to get in first with 'Bags, I . . .' We stood in circles hoping to be picked while a leader counted: 'Eeney, meeny, miney, mo' or 'One potato, two potato, three potato, FOUR!' The last person struck was It. Another rhyme for selection was 'Scissors cuts paper blunts stone'. Once sporty members were distributed evenly among the teams weedy kids were thrown in several at a time for free!

Friday afternoon was always 'free choice' for infants and juniors. Playing shops was a real joy. We made pretend fruit and sweets from plaster of Paris and we bought and sold them with cardboard coins from a stall with a striped awning. There was great dismay at the end of the lesson when we had to return all our goods from the wicker shopping baskets. There were racks of dressing up clothes – girls slapped around in high heels with itchy fur stoles – all of which had to be burned when it was discovered a certain debutante had fleas. The Wendy house was another popular venue. Husbands and wives crowded in the tiny dwelling fighting over the ironing board, the single bed or the miniature cooker. Once a teacher leaned over the wall, caught me cooking at the stove and steered me purposely in the direction of the building bricks.

Roles were rigidly defined in reading schemes in preparation for adulthood. Janet helped mother at the sink while John assisted father repair his car. Daily, our infant teacher would hear the class read, singly or in groups, round her desk. Avidly, we followed the monosyllabic antics of our model family and their dog: 'Nip can run. See Nip run. Run Nip run.'

At the end of the day, or as a special treat, the teacher would read a story and we sat cross-legged on the carpet, spellbound. We could recite from memory chunks of *Three Billy Goats Gruff* and *The Emperor's New Clothes*. Favourites were the mischievous *Gingerbread Man* or the cantankerous *Old Lady Who Lived In A Vinegar Bottle*. We howled over the adventures of *Milly Molly Mandy* and hooted at *Little Black Sambo* (the latter is now relegated to the reserve shelves of the public library, or perhaps even the bonfire, owing to political correctness).

Once a fit-up theatre company arrived and set up their primitive scenery in the school hall. We sat – legs crossed, backs straight – in the round as the young actors presented *Hansel and Gretel*. It was my introduction to theatre and I was enchanted. We could hardly contain our excitement as the mischievous pair came across the cottage made from confectionery in the Magic Wood. Try convinving us that the roof wasn't made from liquorice allsorts, the door from pure milk chocolate and the porch from barley sugar sticks! That wonderful moment when Gretel tricked the Wicked Witch into entering her own oven has lasted a lifetime. I wonder if she's still there?

Christmas gave the opportunity for my own class to act in the Nativity. All the best parts went to teacher's pets but at least I secured a fly-on part as an angel. For weeks I rehearsed the lines: 'Glory to *God* in the highest . . . Glory to God in the *highest* . .' Meanwhile Mum was busy turning a discarded bed sheet into a shining white robe, fashioning wire coathangers into wings and twisting tinsel into the shape of a halo. In the event our play was disastrous: Joseph was sick at the door and Mary knocked Baby Jesus's head off into the makeshift manger. The adults' adoration turned to alarm as the gymnasium form balanced precariously atop step ladders began to sag and the heavenly host were whisked away into the wings without delivering their glad tidings.

Christmas was a time we looked forward to avidly. It took the whole month of December to decorate the classrooms. Pupils abandoned their studies and applied their talents to hanging home made garlands and paper chains. Friezes were team efforts and themes included The Twelve Days of Christmas, I Saw Three Ships, Winter Landscape and Pantomimes. We made decorations for the giant tree standing in a bucket swaddled in crepe paper in the foyer. A crib lit

115

by torches held figures ingeniously formed from toilet rolls. An advent calendar was pinned to the wall and it was a mark of honour to reveal the figure concealed behind closed windows and doors – Angel Gabriel, the Shepherds, the Magi and star attraction – Baby Jesus.

Christmas cards sprinkled with glitter were made for friends in other classes and popped into hand made envelopes stamped with charity seals. A circular postbox appeared, covered with pretend snow, and the contents were regularly sorted and delivered by junior postmen. Our kindly infant teacher paid for ribbons and glitter out of her own money so we could make New Year calendars for our mums. Everywhere was festooned with tissue and crepe paper, tinsel and cotton wool. Noise escalated as excitement mounted.

During the last week we would be escorted class by class into the main hall where we sat on forms against the wall. The teachers organised parlour games – Farmers In His Den, Oranges and Lemons, Musical Chairs, Blind Man's Bluff and Pass The Parcel – played to the accompaniment of a portable Dansette player. Tea was served in the dining hall – huffkins, fish paste sandwiches, fairy cakes and fruit jellies. Father Christmas arrived (our portly caretaker in feeble disguise) to hand out useful gifts of colouring pencils, geometry sets, quiz books, miniature dolls dressed in traditional costume . . . Oranges, apples and bananas were distributed before we were marched off to the cloakroom for

hats, coats, scarves and gloves. My fondest memory of Mongeham School is walking home alone clutching my party goodies one winter evening in the dark.

School dinners, by contrast, were the bane of my life. At midday we washed our hands and filed into the canteen where hard forms knocked against trestle tables presided over by power-crazed junior monitors. 'Hands together and eyes closed.' We stood to chant the soulless:

'ForwhatweareabouttoreceiveLordmakeustrulythankful.'

The weekly menu rarely changed and consisted of combinations of mince, carrots, cabbage and dense gravy. Lumpy potatoes, lumpy swede, lumpy custard. Fridays heralded the speciality of the house – cold, damp, grey fish. A pudding which always caused distress was tapioca (frogspawn) served with brown sugar which infants were convinced came direct from the sand tray. Dinner ladies insisted we ate up every scrap.

Summer term heralded outdoor activities. Football (shirts versus skins) turned to cricket and rounders (girls against boys). Sports Day was the main event. For weeks we practised, divided into teams, on the school field in those long sultry months. Teachers coaxed and coerced their star pupils for the bean bag race, skipping race, sack race, wheelbarrow race, hoop race, three-legged race . . . and endless sprints and relays. Stopwatch, shouts and whistles. Our

117

caretaker, bemused, leisurely smoked his pipe and marked the emerald grass with lime.

Finally, the Great Day came. Proud parents, in floppy hats and floral clothes, with flasks and cameras, jostled for the prime places by the finishing post. A table at the far end under the sycamore trees was laden with cups and trophies, new polished and glistening in the sun.

By now I was proficient in the egg and spoon race and considered myself well up to Olympic standards. Scorning to cheat by adding glue or chewing gum to the spoon I'd practised for hours on our prefab lawn with a pottery egg borrowed from under Gran's broody hen. Overcoming the shyness of appearing in T-shirt and shorts in front of parents, teachers and neighbours, I sped down the track and finished third to thunderous applause.

The final event of the day was the Parents' Race. Acute embarrassment was to be endured as mums and dads ran barefoot, huffing and puffing, gasping and panting, pushing and shoving, towards the winning line. Here was a chance to display open hostility as neighbourly feuds simmered then rose to the boil. On one occasion there was a delicious fight! It was almost a relief to gather around the prize table and listen politely to the visiting celebrity's congratulatory speech relayed fuzzily over the loudspeakers, and to receive the miniature cups, now tied with colourful ribbons, which we knew would lay tarnishing in the stock cupboard for another twelve months.

At the height of the season was the Summer Fair. For weeks every class was industrious in producing items for sale: paper windmills, embroidered bookmarks, pottery ashtrays . . . Mongeham School was turned into a third world

sweat factory. Tables and chairs were carried out the day before on to the school field and bunting was strung across the playground. There was a contingency plan to hold the fete indoors in case of rain.

It was fun seeing the teachers in their sunhats – smiling and coaxing – standing behind their stalls. They looked like they had missed their vocation as shop assistants in Woolworth's. Our field was vast and stalls were neatly spaced. Hand painted notices, flags and streamers flapped in the breeze. There were the bottle stall, fortune teller, bran tub, dart throwing, lucky straws, roll-a-penny, bowling for a pig and all kinds of games of skill and chance.

Special attractions included police dog handlers and junior majorettes interspersed with our own displays of tuneless choirs and skinny gymnasts. A platform held a microphone to announce these events. At times it was unattended. For a dare I mounted the steps and broadcast a welcome 'on behalf of all the pupils' and heard with pleasure my shrill voice reverberate around the field. Did that clip on the ear from the headmistress also register on the public address system?

One section of the field was devoted to a Pets' Corner. There was fierce competition among the pupils to display their pets in hutch, cage or pen. Patrons paid a nominal fee to see their own animals dozing in the sun in unfamiliar surroundings – rabbits, guinea pigs, hamsters, mice, parrots, tortoises. In the event the art teacher's daughter's pony from the local stables stole the show. It gave rides! Even now it beats me how I transported, single handed, the palatial hutch which contained my prize Netherlands dwarf white rabbit, Sugar.

119

Parents' Evening was dreaded by teachers and pupils alike. We worked hard to make an impression and stayed behind to help pin special displays of class-work to the walls. Exercise books were carefully scanned and only best work was placed on top of our shared desks. Mothers in hats and gloves dragged along fathers in their Sunday suits to feign interest in their children's progress. We watched in dismay as nosey neighbours desk-hopped while waiting for the teacher to peruse rival pupils' work.

Schoolwork was far more competitive at that time and streamlining was the current educational trend. Annual school reports presented in minute detail each pupil's position in class for every subject, with teachers' brief comments about effort and attainment: 'Tries hard,' 'Lacks concentration,' 'Could do better . . .' Grammar School was the sole aim of all the parents for their offspring and the Eleven Plus entrance exam loomed over our young lives. I had been dismissed as a Borderline Case.

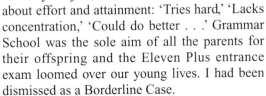

The summer holidays in those days seemed interminable – sunshine, seaside and weeks of freedom. Solemnly, pupils were ushered into the school hall for a farewell service in the late afternoon:

'Lord, dismiss us with thy blessing,
Thanks for mercies past receive;
Pardon all, their faults confessing;
Time that's lost may all retrieve . . .'

The younger kids, me among them, daring to look behind, drawn by the sniffling, studied the faces of the leavers – swats and bullies – tears streaming down their faces.

'Those returning,
Those returning,
Make more faithful than before.'

When it was my turn to stand and sing amongst the back row ('Leavers, omit the final refrain!') I stood resolutely facing forwards, dry-eyed and determined. Whatever lay ahead could never bring such trials and torments as these supposed Happiest Days of My Life.

BUCKET AND SPADE

PERIODICALLY a policeman would visit Mongeham School to warn pupils not to pick up any strange metal objects found on Deal beach. After the war there was a concerted effort by the army to clear the shore of landmines but these were washed up or unearthed well into the next decade. Bulldozers were still working to clear the coast of barbed wire and concrete posts set into the sandhills to deter the possible progress of enemy tanks. Oblivious to these manoeuvres I made the lonely beach at the North End of the town my playground whenever I visited Gran.

One day word went round that a body had been washed ashore. This was a common occurrence in the years after the war yet still a curiosity for kids. We cycled down to the seashore just in time to watch a bobby with a billhook retrieve a bobbing body from the murky water. Another policeman stood by to cover the drowned man with a tarpaulin. For a moment there was real excitement as we huddled in our circle of cycles on the promenade to watch the spectacle. We didn't know many dead people so this was a novelty. After a while it all became a bit boring so we kicked our heels and raced away in the hope of finding some livelier activity.

Who these companions were escapes me now. It was most unusual for me to be in the company of friends when exploring the fishermen's quarter at north

Deal. I had been born here and so was quite content to wander alone along the foreshore watching the fishermen mending their nets, climbing atop the old wooden capstans, clambering over the breakwaters, skimming pebbles or running across the shingle dodging the waves.

The Royal Hotel, where Nelson stayed with Emma one summer prior to Trafalgar, remains the only building on the seafront where there were once many. It effectively divides the foreshore into two halves. Tourists in their coachloads assume that the promenade alongside the pier is the full extent of the seafront whereas the beach continues northwards of The Royal for a further mile. Local residents keep this secret because they regard it exclusively as their domain.

My patch extended northwards as far as Sandown Castle, one of three fortification built by Henry VIII to defend this part of the Kentish coast from invasion from the Continent. Its design reflected the shape of the Tudor rose but only one 'petal' (or bastion) remained after centuries of encroachment by the sea. You could sit on the stone ramparts with your legs dangling over the edge braving the waves which continued to lash the crumbling stonework.

Seagirt was another building remembered with affection by older inhabitants. This was a row of fishermen's cottages having a profusion of dormer windows and gables shrouded in ivy. They stood unusually at right angles to the road but actually on the beach. During the war the building had been forti-

fied and my young imagination converted it into a castle inhabited by knights in shining armour. Seagirt came to an inglorious end. We watched with sadness as it shivered and trembled and with one final sigh of submission slipped forever into the sea.

There were several smaller features of the seafront which I well recall in the 1950s. A wartime sea mine complete with brass detonators stood on the promenade, defused and now

GUINNESS
TIME

serving as a gigantic moneybox for a sailors' charity. A shellfish stall was wheeled early every morning to its prime site by the pier. The white coated vendor enjoyed a brisk trade with his tiny porcelain dishes of cockles, winkles, peeled prawns and gristly whelks swimming in malt vinegar, sweltering in the sun. A public telescope faced seawards and for one penny you were rewarded with a minutes' view of the horizon. Steps were provided for youngsters who couldn't quite reach but the angle of the telescope was still far too steep. When you pulled it down to look through the lens you could see only the sky!

For entertainment a crazy golf course was laid out each summer and the brightly painted obstacles included windmills, churches, oast houses and forts. Miniature clubs steered balls across bridges, through tunnels, over hills and round volcanoes which, I swear, were painted redundant ARP helmets. Then there was a brisk trot along the seafront in an authentic pony and trap – like the one grandad owned. Patrons sat sideways savouring the sights and the salt sea air. A beach photographer recorded all these activities, snapping away at visitors strolling along the prom. Gran, who hated having her photo taken, was proud enough of her grandson to submit to a double portrait on one occasion. Later that evening we sneaked along to the kiosk to have a preview of our picture displayed along with hundreds of identical snaps in the side window.

The Guinness Clock also made its annual appearance on Deal's promenade. This was a replica of the popular musical revolving clock made for the Festival of Britain at Battersea Park in 1951. Fantasy figures rotated, including the Guinness zoo animals and their keeper, when it operated every half hour. There was a spinning sun, I remember, an amusing ostrich, toucans pecking at a tree trunk and the Mad Hatter fishing – every time he caught one fish another appeared from its open mouth! The giant clock attracted tremendous crowds.

Even the deserted North End held a few attractions. There was a sizeable roller skating rink which was quite popular for a time. It was surrounded by a small fairground and an amusement arcade. Further along there was a putting green. In the centre stood a miniature windmill with revolving sails. There was definitely no shortage of things to do at the seaside in the 1950s.

Deal Castle Paddock was railed off for a few months in summer to accommodate children's entertainment. An uncle in a boater, striped blazer, white duck trousers and gold cravat would keep us amused for upwards of an hour, giving parents time to enjoy the seafront in the days when children could be entrusted to the care of perfect strangers. He was wonderfully versatile being a magician, mimic, singer, comic, ventriloquist and tap dancer. It must have seemed to him in those optimistic postwar days only a short dance step away to The Palladium.

A series of ice cream parlours graced the seafront (two remain) and it was a real treat to be bought a cone or wafer to eat while strolling along the beach. Each of the parlours had its own distinctive atmosphere. Deal Beach Parlour was considered modern with its self service counter covered with Vitriolite panels, garish plastic drop ceiling lights, Formica topped rectangular tables, chrome chairs with vinyl seats and hand coloured photographic murals including one showing a toddler in bib and braces and a sunhat licking a dripping ice cream cornet.

Divitos had a loud juke box which attracted rowdy teenagers who lounged around all day in Lloyd Loom chairs drinking coffee, while The Corner Parlour, by contrast, served trays of afternoon tea and expensive Kunzel cakes to the gentry. Tucked away by the bus station was the far less glamourous South Street Parlour, whose window was graced by a plaster advertisement sign of a bathing beauty in a bikini holding up an outsize ice cream cone. When Gran had a little money to spare she would take me inside one of these parlours and slowly sip one cup of milky tea while I savoured an ice cream soda. My envious eyes admired the passing confections – Peach Melba, Banana Longboat, Pineapple Split, Knickerbocker Glory. This last was an immense tall glass filled with chunks of coloured jelly, segments of fruit, generous scoops of ice cream and a scattering of hundreds and thousands.

Afterwards we might stroll for the hundredth time along the pier.

Deal's Victorian pier was breached during the last war by a Dutch motor vessel, the *Nora*. This unlucky cargo vessel was struck by a drifting enemy seamine and subsequently carried northwards by a freak storm where she crashed broadside into the pier. During the early years of the war *Nora* lay upside down on the beach, a pathetic spectacle beside the iron structure she had mortally wounded. Lads used to play on her battered, upturned hull.

Shortly afterwards the crippled pier was blown up by the Royal Engineers because it obstructed the field of fire from coastal guns erected on the seafront after the fall of France. Churchill had been in the area previous to this time, staying at The Royal Hotel, and local rumour asserted that he had personally ordered the demolition, fearing Hitler's troops might mount machine guns on the pierhead to fire on inhabitants on the beach.

For the early part of my childhood a new concrete construction was underway. Deal's new pier was the first to be built since the war and after recent hurricanes remains the only pleasure pier in Kent. A grand opening ceremony took place in November 1957 when a young Prince Philip, Duke of Edinburgh, officially opened the pier attended by the Mayor and Corporation, county dignatories and the band of the Royal Marines. After the Royal Marines had fired a salute the local children rushed forward to hunt for the burning hot spent cartridges.

Deal's pier has remained a constant joy to visitors and townsfolk alike. People take great pleasure in walking along its 1,000 foot length (just a bit longer than SS *Titanic*) for a panoramic view of the shore, ships in The Downs and, on clear days, the coast of France. Apart from a pierhead cafe and some penny slot machines there was little for a child to enjoy when it was first built. The pier remains popular with anglers, however, and at times children's fishing competitions were organised. This was a threefold source of misery to me: handling the bait, killing live fish and eating the catch for breakfast the next morning.

Great excitement was afforded whenever the pleasure steamer, *Royal Daffodil*, arrived from Margate on Sunday afternoons to take passengers on a brief cruise along the English Channel. The fare for the round trip was 6s/6d. There was talk of extending these excursions to France but the whole exercise was abandoned since the ship constantly hit the lower deck of the pier!

The Goodwin Sands lie off Deal. These treacherous sandbanks are twelve miles long, five miles wide and four miles offshore. They lie concealed directly in the line of shipping passing through the narrowest stretch of the Channel. Over the centuries they have claimed thousands of ships and sailors and for this reason they are known as the shippe-swallower.

For most of the year The Goodwins are completely covered by water and their shape is constantly changing at every tide making them impossible to chart with accuracy. For this reason their presence is ringed by three lightships and a series of marker buoys whose twinkling lights can be seen distinctly from the shore. On murky nights the mournful wail of the foghorns alarm visitors who conjure up fearful imaginations of sea monsters.

At high tide the Goodwin Sands are completely covered but during exceptionally low tides in early summer the sandbanks are revealed. The soft white sand hardens rapidly in the hot sunshine to enable folk to stroll across the shoals. Intrepid boatmen have been known to play cricket, football and golf among the wrecks, watched by whirling seagulls and basking seals on this precarious adventure playground mid-Channel. In modern times hovercraft trips to The Goodwins have become a popular event to benefit local charities.

Less pleasantly, distressed ships in freak storms throughout history have drifted towards The Goodwins where they have been held fast on the sands. If they can be rescued immediately there is a slim chance of survival for the stricken craft, but more likely a vessel is held fast in the grip of The

Goodwins. Over successive tides a vessel breaks its back, slinks on its side and sinks irretrievably beneath the waves.

Because The Goodwins present such a hazard to shipping there have been three lifeboat stations along the coast at Deal, Walmer and Kingsdown. Walmer Station, the first to be the established, is the only one that remains. During my childhood it was a popular walk along The Strand as far as the lifeboat house and back home in time for tea. Walmer was one of the three beach launching stations in the country – the others were at Aldeburgh, in Suffolk, and Dungeness, in Kent – but the lifeboat has now been replaced by a fast inshore inflatable rubber rescue dinghy.

Throughout the Second World War and the immediate postwar period *The Charles Dibdin (Civil Service No 2)* was on station at Walmer. It saved more than 400 lives during the quarter of a century it remained in service. This noble motor driven vessel was replaced in 1959 by the *Charles Dibdin (Civil Service No 32)* whose dedication by the Archbishop of Canterbury was another occasion for celebration.

Launching the lifeboat was an exciting event. Distress signals fired from a ship in trouble would be answered from the shore by a series of maroons discharged from the lifeboat station. These rockets, whose retort could be heard throughout the town, summoned the lifeboat crew. A first rocket indicated stand by, a second meant launch while a possible third would summon a doctor. Volunteer lifeboatmen would race out of houses or pubs along the seafront and flag down passing motorists who were often perfect strangers. A passenger would surrender a seat to allow the lifeboatman to be driven at speed to the lifeboat house.

There the *Charles Dibdin* would be turned on its swivel base and tilted ready to launch. The first eight lifeboatmen to arrive formed the crew and they would hastily don their lifejackets, oilskins and sou'westers as they clambered aboard. Locals would hold the ropes of the oily wooden skids to enable the lifeboat to speed down the makeshift slipway and hit the waves, froth flying in all directions. Often the red flares from the distressed vessel would be still fading as Walmer Lifeboat sped to its rescue.

'All aboard the Skylark!' An elderly boatmen in cap and blazer, hands in his pockets in a jaunty style, would stand on the prom and drum up passengers for a trip round the Goodwins. On sunny afternoons Mum might succumb to his suggestion so we would pick our way up the rickety ramp at the waters' edge and clamber into the craft. The boat was overloaded and so low in the water it felt as if we might be tipped into the sea as *The Skylark* rocked to and fro with the tide. If you leaned over the side you could trail your fingers in the foam as the boat chug-chugged past the pier and round one of the buoys marking the

western edge of the Goodwins.

When we returned, the shoreline with its myriad houses, each having a different arrangement of doors and windows, roofs and chimneys, backed up with the turrets and spires of churches beyond, and the concealed features of the three castles, lifeboat station and timeball tower, never ceased to delight.

The shore extended further out to sea – or so it seemed to me – when I was a child. What is certain is that fishing boats were beached in profusion and extended from Walmer Strand to the North End in an (almost) continuous line. I could recite their names as I skipped along the prom – *Gipsy King, Carefree, Golden Spray, Lady Jane, Sunbeam* . . . Two white painted clinker built launches with amusing names stood side-by-side near the pier: *If Not* and *Why Not.*

At the far end of the promenade adjacent, to Deal Castle, was a grandiloquent building, The Queens Hotel. Originally it had been called The South Eastern since the hotel had been built by that railway company for its customers when the line reached Deal towards the end of the last century. Above the central arch appeared two angels – one supporting a galleon, the other a steam locomotive. A long conservatory extended along the entire facade broken only by the impressive porch, and here dined the gentry enjoying silver service with a view of the silvery sea. Feathered hats bobbed among the potted palms and we knew, Gran and I, it was as much as we dared to cross the road and peruse the exorbitant menu.

Beach picnics whenever friends or relatives stayed was more our style of dining *al fresco*. We would march down to the seafront armed with travel rugs, towels, picnic basket, tan lotion, sun hats and wasp repellent as though engaged in military exercise. Deal has a shingle beach which faces east and therefore turns it back to the sun every afternoon. Windshields were useless as they cannot be pegged into pebbles, so we huddled around the rusty groins

130

seeking protection from the biting coastal winds.

Mother bravely donned a one-piece swimsuit with a rubber bathing cap prettily decorated with imitation flowers. Tentatively, she picked her way across the sharp stones like a fakir on live coals. She would attempt a few strokes close inshore, desperately trying to convince us that the water was really quite warm. Father gamely rolled up his trouser legs, kicked off his sandals, knotted his handkerchief over his peeling sunburnt head and paddled his bunioned feet in the surf.

There was then the palaver of changing on a crowded seafront. We covered our bodies from head to toe with rugs and towels as we struggled out of wet swimwear into casual clothes. Mine was the most modest family on the entire beach. Before the sun went down Mother would disappear to Gran's house and reappear with a tray of refreshments. We munched thick cucumber sandwiches and sipped sweet tea poured from a large brown teapot with a chipped spout.

An Ensign box camera provided a feast of fun. Father loaded a film onto the squeaky spool and taped the sides to ensure no light got in to fog the negative. There were two viewing windows so that you got a clear impression of your subject whether you held it horizontally or vertically. Careful not to shake the heavy camera, Father stood with baited breath until there was a clunk indicating that he had completed one exposure.

Mother had the idea that we could take some trick snapshots, and tried to organise our relatives in ludicrous poses. She laid a travel rug on the pebbles and got one person to lie underneath with just his or her head exposed and another to lie with just the feet sticking out the other end thus creating the illusion of an extremely long person. A second idea was to get one person to stand on another person's shoulders, lifting up the rug to disguise two bodies, making it look like it was a very tall person. That seemed to have exhausted all the possibilities so Father took shots of passing boats and seagulls on the breakers. Film came in reels of twelve exposures, which were expensive to develop. By the time our film was returned from the chemist's several years later we had quite forgotten what all the fun had been about.

The adults, realising an only child needed to be entertained, thoughtfully provided me with beach toys. After all, it was far easier to spend money on a mardy kid rather than give it undivided attention. Thus I found myself armed with a gaily decorated tin bucket and spade, an assortment of plastic moulds in the shape of marine life and – oh, yes! – a shrimping net to amuse myself on a shingle beach! Even the large colourful beach ball – an essential part of seaside activity in the 1950s – was commandeered by the grown-ups.

The problem was I could not swim. How a human body manages to stay afloat in water still baffles me and although I had lessons for years at my secondary school I still cannot swim one stroke. One uncle was a confirmed believer in the throw-'em-in-at-the-deep-end school of swimming. To be fair

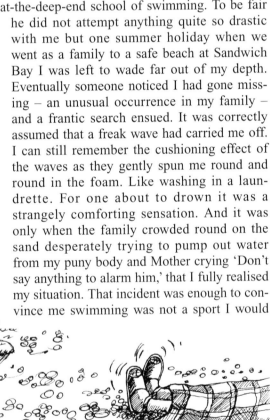

he did not attempt anything quite so drastic with me but one summer holiday when we went as a family to a safe beach at Sandwich Bay I was left to wade far out of my depth. Eventually someone noticed I had gone missing – an unusual occurrence in my family – and a frantic search ensued. It was correctly assumed that a freak wave had carried me off. I can still remember the cushioning effect of the waves as they gently spun me round and round in the foam. Like washing in a laundrette. For one about to drown it was a strangely comforting sensation. And it was only when the family crowded round on the sand desperately trying to pump out water from my puny body and Mother crying 'Don't say anything to alarm him,' that I fully realised my situation. That incident was enough to convince me swimming was not a sport I would ever master. In future I was relegated to the role of observer and guardian of the towels whilst my schoolmates swam races round the pier.

Deal Regatta took place over three days in July and was the most important event on the south coast. For weeks members of the Rowing Club (founded by our family benefactor, Sir Ernest, Mr Justice Charles) practised in their sculls – singles, pairs and fours – sporting purple and grey colours. On one occasion they sank before my eyes! Teams from rival resorts fiercely competed by rowing and sailing in skiffs and punts. There were novelty races, too, to entertain spectators – raft race, float race, model yacht race and a dramatic rescue race to an offshore burning galley. Today only two of these prized Deal working craft remain in local museums, *Saxon King* and *Undaunted*.

Over the long weekend the town was *en fête*. Abundant activities took place on Walmer Green including a glamourous grandmother competition, bonny baby competition, treasure hunt, high diving into a shallow tank of water, climbing a greasy pole and a rather alarming event held in a canvas tank called Neptune's Court. There were town criers, firework displays, band concerts and carnival dances. These festivities culminated in a grand carnival. The Royal Marines marched ahead of a lively procession through the town composed of decorated lorries, prams and cycles, children wearing fancy dress, massed bands, tradesmen's vehicles and finally our own Beauty Queen with her attendants riding on a float pulled by the Sea Scouts. Hurrah! Hurrah! I'd place my wooden stool on the pavement in the High Street to watch the parade in comfort and then, when the last float passed, race onto the seafront to catch it all over again!

Deal's regatta was accompanied by Forrest's Funfair which stretched as far as the eye could see along the entire length of the promenade. Main attractions occupied the North End while juvenile rides were built separately between The Royal Hotel and the pier. This annual event was the highlight of the town's calendar. It provided seasonal work for everyone: tough youths manned the rides while refined ladies opened the windows of their houses to serve teas

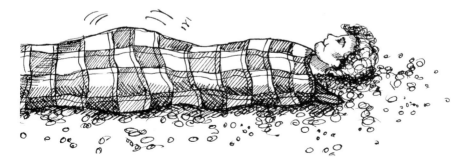

directly onto the seafront.
This was the zenith of
my year. Mum and Dad
would book an unadven-
turous holiday staying
with the relatives in Derby
or a fortnight's stint at
Butlins, leaving me in the
charge of Gran. I would
be up at dawn watching
the fairground trailers
arrive and the showmen
constructing the attrac-
tions. On the first day the
big rides took shape; on
the second day the round-
stalls and sideshows. I
was mesmerised by the
magic of the 'now you see
it; now you don't' aspect
of our funfair taking shape
Before your very eyes.

When the fair officially opened I never wanted to go on anything but was perfectly content to savour the sights and the sounds, the colour and the movement of a traditional travelling fair.

Big rides included the skids (or the waltzer), the dodgems and the motorbike
speedway, consisting of wooden cutouts that undulated round the circular
track at rapid speed. Once, I think, there was a helter skelter. But the octopus
drew the greatest crowd. Girls screamed and clung to their boyfriends as the
tight tubs spun round alarmingly. Its iron tentacles rose and fell and every so
often appeared to be throwing courting couples over the breakwaters and out
to sea.

Centrepiece was the carousel. This was a wonderful Victorian confection:
galloping horses, snarling bears, crowing cockerels and graceful gondolas.
Three-abreast. There were silver barley sugar posts, ornate rounding boards,
patriotic flags and a red-and-white striped canvas top. The carving and the
paintwork of the figures were captivating. In the centre was an organ decorated with flamboyant mirrors and automaton figures that clashed cymbals and
banged drums as punched music sheets concertinaed to play selections from
memorable stage shows. This magical roundabout never stopped – you had to

hop onto the curved steps sharpish when it slowed down to catch the ride – but constantly rotated in a clockwise direction transporting the lucky patrons on to paradise.

Round stalls with striped canvas tops and bright coloured lights filled in the gaps. There were games of chance and skill – roll-a-penny, ring-a-duck, lucky straws, darts and hoop-la! Prizes ranged from cuddly toys to cigarette packets, puppets with painted chalk heads to live goldfish which you proudly carried home in a plastic bag. Along the sides stood the shooting gallery and coconut shy. Mother was skilled at throwing balls into the buckets. The trick, she confided, was to throw 'em in sideways.

One of my favourite attractions was the wall of death. This was a circular wooden wall ridden vertically by daredevil motorcyclists. They rode vintage bikes at high speed to perform stunts – riding backwards, sitting sideways, standing up, steering with their feet and generally clambering about the vehicle – held fast to the track by centrifugal force. Patrons climbed the surrounding scaffolding to peer over the top, which was equally dangerous, since if a motorcyclist miscalculated the wheels would surely decapitate the audience.

Occasionally there was a glimpse inside the showmen's wagons. Here was luxury! Sumptuously furnished, the caravans sparkled with etched mirrors, oil lamps and frosted glass windows. Mobile stalls tempted customers with hot dogs, bags of peanuts, candy floss whipped up in rotating tubs from spun sugar and bright red sticky toffee apples. Treasures on sale included kiss-me-kwik hats, glitter balls filled with sawdust which bounced back and forth on elastic and novelty balloons that slipped from your hand to fly over the fairground before vanishing over the sea.

Sideshows stretched far down the North End. Popular booths were the freak show, aquarium and striptease. But nothing could beat the excitement of the boxing booth. On a raised platform in front of a striped tent stood a barker who rang a bell at the sound of which appeared a fairground giant stripped to the waist, arms folded, muscles bulging, silently defying the crowd. In a mining town this was the ultimate challenge to masculinity.

Word went round that one of our burly young miners had decided to fight and this would ensure a stampede. The tent bulged to capacity while outside loudspeakers relayed the commentary. Fists flew in the makeshift roped ring and spectators shouted their encouragement. There was acute disappointment whenever the miner lasted only a few rounds. To compensate we told ourselves that for sure the fight was fixed, it had definitely been rigged, undoubtedly our lad had been paid to lose. Thus our esteem and our corporate manhood remained intact. At least for another year.

At the end of the fortnight chalked boards appeared advertising for strong

135

labourers to help with the pull down. On the Saturday evening towards midnight Forrest's fair would begin to pack up – first the juvenile rides, then the
sideshow attractions and finally the big rides. The carousel turned for the last
time, the coloured lights dimmed, the stirring music faded. Generators provided fierce arc lights for the workmen to begin in earnest. I stayed until the bitter
end. No-one bothered this shy lad leaning against the seaside shelter watching,
dismayed, as our precious fair was dismantled and loaded onto lorries. By
morning there would be no sign of the fair apart from the litter and the chalk
rings indicating where the rides had stood.

On Sunday evenings in July and August Gran would lead me by the hand along the promenade south of The Royal. There she would commandeer the bleak Edwardian shelter by laying coats across all the timber seats to reserve them for her friends who would arrive at intervals. Promptly at eight o'clock after their service at The Citadel, the Salvation Army would march in procession and reform in a circle on the windy prom. More wonderful entertainment!

A bonnetted lassie would hand out faded yellow hymn sheets and optimistically swing a collection tin. Gran's friends proffered the odd coin. The band played stirring anthems, their polished instruments glinting in the setting

sun while a straggle of shivering bathers joined in the chorus. One devout convert would tell how he first met the Lord, his fervent words borne away by the chilling breeze. A final prayer, a gathering of music sheets, sincere smiles and the evangelists stood at ease.

Onward Christian Soldiers. Gran and I walked home along the seafront past the illuminations – strings of gaudy coloured lightbulbs linked the lampposts – and along Middle Street to Redan. Gaslight and shadows. The stars shone their brightest, cheered by our singing, and a harvest moon rose like a gold sovereign held by a smuggler over the sea. We tried to identify the constellations and the planets and admired the recent attempts by scientists to conquer outer space. Orbiting Sputniks, we knew, were to blame for interfering with the weather but would they find life on the moon?

MINER'S LAMP

MORGAN Jones, my grandfather, known to the family as Pop, hailed from Pontypridd, a large mining town near Cardiff, mid-Glamorgan. A miner, he had journeyed to the north of England to work in the coal mines of Yorkshire. There he had married my Gran, Jessie, a shy girl who worked in a cotton mill in Manchester.

Presumably Pop had become involved in the conflicts of the General Strike of 1926 when the striking miners were locked out of their collieries. Fresh opportunities presented themselves when the Kent coalfield was opened up in the mid 1920s. Pop travelled south – walking all the way – and secured work at Betteshanger Colliery, near Dover.

Deal folk did not welcome the miners. They were suspicious of their strange ways and wary of their accents which included Scottish, Yorkshire, Nottinghamshire and Derbyshire. At times there was open hostility between the two communities – north and south – who were only united at the outbreak of war when they fought a common enemy.

Pop's immediate problem was to find suitable accommodation for his wife and two children, my mother, Hilda, and her older brother, Sidney. Discrimination was rife among landladies from the North End of Deal whose advertisements firmly stated: 'No miners need apply'. Yet Pop was fortunate. A chance encounter coupled with his ability to socialise with anyone without regard to class or status secured a lifelong family friend and champion in a local dignatory.

Sir Ernest Charles was the town's greatest benefactor. A pipe smoking, bald and bespectacled bachelor, the retired judge was admired for his geniality and generosity. He recognised that the youth of the town lacked recreational facilities and so he encouraged sporting activities by presenting the Charles Sports Ground to Deal Town Football Club, and he founded The Deal, Walmer and Kingsdown Amateur Rowing Club.

Sir Ernest lived in a grand residence on the seafront, Bruce House, and he was often to be seen strolling along the foreshore pausing to chat to the local boatmen. And so it was one fine sunny day that he happened to share a bench on the promenade with my grandfather, who engaged him in conversation.

Pop mentioned the animosity aroused by the arrival of the miners and his own plight in attempting to find lodgings for his young family. Sir Ernest immediately offered assistance. He took Pop to look at a grand upstairs apartment in Redan, a large house in Middle Street, which backed on to the spacious garden of Bruce House. Although the accommodation was vast it was offered at a peppercorn rent. When the family travelled down from Yorkshire they were surprised to find their new home cleaned, furnished and stocked with food as a welcoming gift.

The mining community irrevocably changed the face of this quiet seaside town over the next decade. A sprawling housing estate was constructed at the top of Mill Hill to accommodate the miners and two schools – South Deal Primary (1934) and Deal Central Secondary (1936) – were built in Mill Road. Food shops stocked cheaper cuts of meat and portions of cheese strictly reserved for the miners while overalls and pit boots appeared in the windows of outfitters.

Competitiveness in sport brought the tough northern lads to the fore. Sidney Jones was one of these lads who distinguished himself by winning medals for the rowing club. Success ensured a wide circle of friends. He was fond of his younger sister, my mother, although he often teased her by chasing her with his pet white mice. Despite her loving family Mum must have been a lonely child. Certainly, she suffered deep humiliation when neighbours called their children indoors rather than allow them to mix with a common miner's daughter.

Redan is an almost symmetrical double-fronted Georgian house, white rendered, with shy dormers and an immense lantern lit porch. Ale boards were displayed on the first floor for this had once been a hotel named after a fort outside Sevastopol, stormed by British troops during the Crimean War. Previously it had been a temperance hotel, The Clifton, boasting landscaped

139

tea gardens with a concert hall and a bandstand beside the sea.

A cracked and faded Victorian picture postcard shows summer visitors taking tea in these popular gardens. A large circle of ladies sip tea from china cups set out on a starched linen tablecloth presided over by a portly matron heavily dressed in bombasine while a proud mother nurses her infant alongside a bassinet. A moustachioed waiter in straw hat and waistcoat, a napkin over his arm, steers a tray of non-alcoholic beverages between the tables and deck chairs. He is watched intently by a parrot in a large cage hidden among the decorative ferns.

Redan was now a scout hall. You could watch the scouts going through their paces, swinging Indian clubs and signalling with semaphore flags, if you peered through a skylight from the upstairs kitchen window. They occupied two large rooms on either side of a long, narrow passage which led to an inner door giving access to the living quarters. Later these downstairs rooms were converted into an antiques showroom which held packed auctions at intervals.

A dark stairwell led directly into the landing – you came up straight through the floor! – where a run of sash windows looked out on to the lawn behind a high wall where the celebrated tea gardens had once been. Step down from the landing and a short passage led to four rooms – the kitchen, the sitting room and two bedrooms. All these rooms were large with high ceilings and angular walls. They were sparsely furnished, too, for my grandparents could afford only basic furniture.

Once, when I was a child, Gran inherited cumbersome colonial style furniture which filled up the landing. There was a marble topped and serpentine fronted chiffonier with ornate carving; a slender oval table on a single stand and a tiny bureau with a let-down writing flap. Such items would fetch an immense price at auction today but Gran scorned them for being ugly and old fashioned. Strange to think that we considered ourselves so poor we could afford only antique furniture!

The first bedroom one encountered was occupied by Gran. None of its four walls was true, making it difficult to furnish. There was an Edwardian bamboo table beside the duck's nest fire grate and an iron bed with brass nobs that tended to fall off during the night. It gave you quite a fright! A most curious feature was the borrowed light – a tall sash window which one might assume gave a view of the garden but in fact looked directly back into the landing. You could lie in bed and watch people arrive and depart without them realising.

A second flight of steep stairs led to the attic. This consisted of three awkward rooms with impossibly sloping ceilings. You had to struggle to stand upright as you passed from room to room. It was here that I was born in a back bedroom so tucked away that you might think no-one would ever find you. Home births, even difficult ones such as mine, were a fairly common occurrence in post-war Britain.

My parents had these rooms as a flat when they were married. Later on Gran rented them out to married couples for a little extra income. Goodness knows how they managed. There was a modest kitchen but no bathroom and the toilet was shared. This was a tiny room at the end of the dim passage which I dreaded using at night. Gran would light a candle for me to place beside the blue willow pattern washbasin on a pine stand. There was difficulty enough sitting on the icy seat, trousers around my ankles, reaching for the iron chain.

The sitting room, warm and comfortable in the afternoons, was Gran's domain. It was papered with an oppressive pattern of autumn leaves with a matching frieze below the picture rail. A pair of sentimental coloured prints hung along one wall showing an Edwardian lady exercising two hunting dogs and a tearful girl crying over her homework comforted by her pet dogs; they had cost Gran a halfpenny each plus coupons from Mazawattee tea. A portrait showing a dour Victorian gent with a goatee beard hung in a recess. Obviously an ancestor, we never knew who, but Gran venerated him too much to replace him with a lighter picture.

The room was furnished in primitive Art Deco. The floor was covered with a thick carpet having an orange and brown geometrical design with zigzag borders. There was a suite of angular brown leather armchairs, a sideboard with doors that would never stay closed and a dining table placed between the two sash windows which looked out on to Middle Street.

Gran's wedding photograph, bound by passe-partout, was nailed crookedly to the wall. It was a truly mournful sepia scene with Gran, unrecognisable as a young bride, in a dowdy white frock tied with a cumbersome bow. She looked uncertain of the future and of happiness.

By the fireplace stood a pair of heavy spelter Edwardian figures representing Work and Play. They had been a wedding gift from the workers at her mill in Manchester. She cried when she was presented with them. She had asked for a clock.

The open fire was surrounded by a varnished mantelpiece with twin carvings of lions' heads. Their open mouths snarled threateningly at you as you sank into the deep leather armchairs. In summer the fireplace was concealed by a screen featuring a crinoline lady made from silver paper mounted behind dark painted glass. Tinsel pictures were a popular art form during the war years. Gran was hooking a hearthrug with rust coloured wool over the years but it was never quite finished. When she died we threw it away.

Running almost the entire length of one wall was a glass fronted pine cup-

142

board. On rainy days it was fascinating to explore for it held wonderful treasures: a scholar's mortarboard, real lead pencils, rowing club trophies . . . Dusty tomes included a set of encyclopaedias with outdated information, mother's discarded Pitman shorthand typing course notebooks and *Grimms Fairy Tales* whose monochrome pictures I improved with wax crayons. Most intriguing were mystery objects from a magician's box of tricks. Pop was something of a conjurer, it transpired, because he used to tour the working men's clubs giving performances of his skill.

There was a wooden cup and ball (the ball disappeared and reappeared at will); two blocks of wood attached by a rope (when you cut the rope you were still able to pass it through both blocks when they were held together) and a set of iron rings which, if struck sharply at a certain point, linked as if by magic. Years later I infuriated a magician at the local theatre when he invited any little boy or girl on to the stage to hold the same style rings whilst he joined them one by one. When he turned his back to me to address the audience I sneakily linked all the chains together myself! His theatrical smile faded to a scowl which only I could see.

Morgan Jones was a fiery Welshman with a strong lyrical accent which he retained all his life, and a shiny bald head which he polished daily with an onion. He was fiercely patriotic and named his mongrel Monty in honour of the war leader, General Montgomery. He was also disgracefully prejudiced. He once shouted at a Pakistani bus conductor: 'Go back to your own country,' to the embarrassment of passengers on a London bus.

But he was indulgent towards his grandson. I have few memories of him but one is when he arrived at our prefab over Christmas when I was four years old to present me with a wooden stool. Its varnished legs bore utility marks and its seat was made of red raffia. Another occasion was when I laid out his prize

143

collection of 78rpm records on the kitchen floor and danced wildly around them in imitation of an African native. He sat watching this mystifying entertainment and roared with laughter even though I cracked the family favourite, Jingle Bells.

On early shifts at the coal mine, Pop never forgot to place his pocket watch in a protective brass container with a glass aperture that revealed the dial which he hung on his belt to give maximum protection whilst working on the coal face. Gran, meanwhile, would pack a stout metal tin with his lunch – invariably thick crusts of bread and a slab of cheese – known as snap.

Gran could hardly be called a cook. Pop never complained at what she served him. His preferences were modest to say the least. Favourite were chunks of bread dropped into warm milk (which he called sops) and an orange sliced, sprinkled with sugar and eaten with brown bread and dripping. Miners lost the taste for butter since it went rancid in sandwiches down the mines.

It was intriguing to watch Pop shave in the morning. First he whipped up a lather with a soap stick in an enamel shaving mug and then he daubed the froth over his face with a squirrel brush. Carefully he unfolded his cutthroat razor which he sharpened on a leather strop kept hanging beside the kitchen sink. Pouting in the chipped mirror, he held his face taut as, with firm upward strokes, he chased his chin. When finished he dabbed the smooth skin with a hot damp towel making sure to give a nod of approval to his reflection.

Pop's brass miner's lamp remains a family treasure since it encapsulates memories of my characterful grandfather. Safety lamps were issued to deputies and overmen leading teams of workmen along the narrow roadways of the coal face. When air samples were tested and the speck of yellow flame from the flatwick spirit lamp turned to a blueish spire it gave a clear indication of the presence of lethal methane gas known as Firedamp. If the flame was extinguished when the lamp was held close to the ground it warned of a dangerous mixture of gases combined with a reduction of oxygen known as Blackdamp. A miner who was tempted to snatch a rest might fall asleep and never wake up. When Pop retired from the Betteshanger Colliery due to ill health he failed to return his lamp to the lamp room and thus we acquired an heirloom.

During his lifetime Pop's pride and joy was his pony and trap. This was a novel form of transport so late in the 1950s and it caused comment and consternation as it whipped in and out of the motor traffic in the town. Pop took his daughter, smartly dressed in her New Look coat, for jaunts along the seafront and once there was a whole family excursion to the countryside to take tea with an elderly couple who lived at Sholden Bank. Water had to be drawn from a well before the kettle could be filled but soon it was steaming on the hob and afternoon tea was served in a gloomy parlour. Pop was heartbroken when he had to forfeit the pair through illness – the trap was auctioned and Tommy the pony put out permanently to graze.

Pop was indulgent towards his son and daughter but even so he ruled them with a rod of iron. He was headstrong and unorthodox in his methods of discipline. Once Sidney was inexplicably rude to Gran, wounding her deeply. Pop said nothing but ominously disappeared from the house. When he returned several hours later he had somehow managed to obtain two pairs of boxing gloves. He took his son into the bedroom, locked the door and they fought it out. Man-to-man. Never again was Gran insulted by her tough young son.

In truth she doted on him. Sidney Jones was clever enough to win a scholar-

ship to Sir Roger Manwood's, an exclusive grammar school in Sandwich. In those days even if bright children were awarded places in selective schools it did not follow that their families would allow them to attend simply because they could not afford the cost of the uniform nor fares for travel. But Gran was a firm believer in education and was prepared to make sacrifices to ensure her son's attendance.

Sidney took a paper round to aid finances. He would get up at dawn to collect the bulging sack of newspapers. Gran would secretly meet him round the corner and while he got ready for school she would deliver the papers herself.

Then there was the incident of Job's bed. Mother, as a young girl, had set her heart on a modern bed which she had admired in the window of the furnishing store known as Job's. Pop decided to treat her so he went into the showroom to enquire about hire purchase. The assistant recognised Pop as a miner, laughed in his face and spoke loudly in front of customers, 'You will never afford to keep up the payments'. Pop stormed out of the shop, drew out all his savings, threw the money on to the counter and commanded Job's obnoxious assistant: 'Deliver my daughter's bed at once!'

Hire purchase had become an acceptable form of transaction for the lower classes in the early 1950s. The abolition of purchase tax and the reduction of income tax gave a certain boost to luxury. All the same the man as breadwinner had to sign the papers for the deal to become legal. One thing at a time was the rule regarding hp in our family, although some friends and neighbours were known to furnish their entire prefabs on the 'never-never'.

The Second World War fragmented the tightly-knit Jones family. Mother, who had led such a sheltered life, joined the WAAF and relished the companionship of service life. She faced danger only once, she said, when a stray German plane machine-gunned her as she returned one day to barracks. She dived into a ditch and returned safely to base with laddered stockings and muddied uniform. The pilot swooped so low she could see his grinning face, for

146

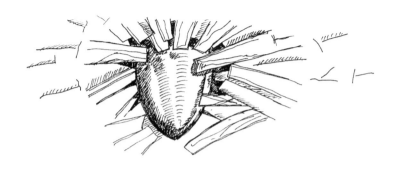

luckily he had only intended giving her a fright.

Pop, who had enlisted in the Welsh Fusiliers during the Great War, now toured the south with Gran in the NAAFI. They spoiled the troops whom they regarded as their extended family. At times they returned to war torn Deal which was directly in the  line of fire from the coastal guns of France. Once they were both staring out of a window on the seafront when a shell exploded on the beach and splintered all the panes of glass.

Another time Gran returned home in deep distress. A stray bomb had fallen through the roof of Clarabuts, a department store packed with shoppers in the High Street. Miraculously, it did not explode for it would have caused tremendous loss of life and devastation. Conscripted munitions workers in Germany sometimes managed to sabotage bombs by making up their weight with soil or sand. In true British tradition Clarabuts displayed its very own UXB guarded by a Royal Marine for the duration of the war as window dressing.

Throughout her life Gran remembered the throb of V1s or Doodlebugs as they flew relentlessly across the Channel to fall indiscriminately in Kent. All the time you heard their drone you knew you were safe, she explained. Everyone dreaded the moment when the engine cut out for these pilotless planes spiralled to drop their explosives within seconds.

At the start of hostilities Sidney enlisted in the Royal Signals and received initial training at Aldershot before being transferred to the infamous Catterick Camp in Yorkshire. When news was received of his promotion to Lance Corporal and imminent posting to Burma a hastily-arranged wedding to his

149

fiancée, Pearl, took place at St George's Church in Deal. At Deal Railway Station the tearful Jones family bade farewell to their son, brother or husband secretly fearing that he might not safely return to England. From the Officers' Training School at Bangalore Sidney Jones soon wrote to say that he had been promoted to Second Lieutenant and was about to join the 3rd Gurkha Rifles stationed at the foot of the Himalayas in northern India.

Periodically, my grandparents received air mail letters stamped by the official censor, bringing news of their son 15,000 miles away fighting the Japanese.

Agra, 24th July 1943: I was posted on active service up where the jungle is. You can guess where. One sees the Rising Sun periodically. We saw it one morning and made it set rather quickly but got into a bit of a mess ourselves. They were four or five to one of us and I lost a lot of my boys. It rather knocked me up inside. Next day I was on my way to Brigade H.Q. when I hit a wire stretched across the road breast high. I came off my motor cycle and woke up in base hospital . . . I was damned lucky. Just my arm and leg broken and a couple of ribs. Just wasn't born to die young, I suppose. Touch wood.

There was a family celebration several months afterwards when relatives gathered for Morgan and Jessie Jones' silver wedding anniversary. A wartime spread had been laid out in the church hall and a cake with a fake iced top baked specially for the occasion. A distant uncle had been delegated to read the congratulatory telegrams piled high on the buffet table. In mid-flow he realised that he was reading a stray pencilled 'Priority' telegram from the Foreign Office at Whitehall: *'Deeply regret to inform you of report received from an Indian Theatre of War that Lieut S Jones 3rd Gurkha Rifles was killed in action.'*

Pearl could never adjust to a husband serving abroad in the army and her letters were full of recriminations followed by meaningful silences. Distance lent disenchantment. Yet she was heartbroken by Sidney's death. For years Pearl kept in touch with my family, sending affectionate letters which dwindled to cards at birthdays and Christmas. A long absence was followed by news of her remarriage. The war tore many lovers apart.

At Redan there were still a few poignant mementos of Lieutenant Sidney Jones who had been killed instantly by an enemy shell in Burma. Tucked under the stairs was a canvas washstand, a drawstring kitbag and a folding camp bed. In cupboards and drawers were a brass transmitter for telegraphing Morse code; a ceremonial cane with a silver top; a rare one shilling note issued by the British Military Authority, presumably as part of a soldier's wages, and a single piece of silver Maundy money from the reign of George II found in his uniform pocket – a lucky mascot which missed its mark.

When I was born I was clearly a replacement in Gran's eyes for her beloved son but Mum firmly resisted calling me Sidney. All her life Gran cosseted me although my parents would never allow me to become the sole centre of attention. Indeed Mum's approach to her only baby could be alarmingly casual at times. Rationing was coming towards an end and Mother heard of bargains galore available at the Co-Op. She returned home laden with delicacies from the store which she proudly displayed on the kitchen table. Later – much later – Gran happened to enquire where her grandson was. Baby Gregory had been left amidst all the excitement of the sales in his pram outside Deal's Co-Op for well over an hour!

As a baby I was neither christened nor baptised but dedicated – handed back to God – at the Glynn Vivian Miners' Mission which served the large mining community at Mill Hill. My parents were mindful of our family patron, Sir Ernest, and they were careful to include among my names that of Charles. Gran was a true Christian although she would never align herself with one particular sect but preferred to attend meetings in turn at the Methodist, Baptist or Congregationalist churches. She drew the line at extremists, however, and shunned services at the Spiritualist church since one of her elderly acquaintances, when filled with the spirit, rolled around in raptures on the floor. Our family was never particularly religious although Gran's quiet dedication shone through.

Once a year relatives from Wales visited Gran for an extended holiday. Uncle

151

Jack was the spitting image of Pop in looks and character and his sardonic humour was relished by the entire family. Aunty Beattie was a fat and florid matron full of anecdote and gossip, while Mother's cousin, Arthur, a confirmed bachelor, was friendly, entertaining and considered a good-looker despite his mouthful of black and broken teeth. He worked in an iron foundry producing chains and anchors for large ships at Swansea.

The attraction of visiting Deal was fishing from the pier so there was always a haul of sprats, codling and mackerel served fresh for breakfast, lunch, tea and supper. Although this one-way visit from Pop's relations was welcome company for a youngster, it imposed increasing hardship on Gran who reluctantly was forced to put a stop to their annual free holiday by the sea. Alas, we never heard from our Welsh relatives again.

One evening, perhaps when I was four or five years old, I was escorted by my parents into the sitting room at Redan to take a farewell leave of Granddad. I had been put to bed in the adjacent bedroom but was unable to sleep because of Pop's deep chesty cough and struggle to breathe. In hushed tones I scampered across Pop's makeshift bed to kiss him goodbye. And as I passed the open fire it scorched the back of my knees. Odd to think that it was this same coal fire that had killed Pop, for he succumbed to the lung disease silicosis, to which miners were prone.

That night Pop died and for days and weeks and months afterwards the house was cold and silent. Gran was left alone in Redan without so much as a widow's pension from the heartless Coal Board which adjudged that her husband's illness was caused partly whilst working in the independent mines of Wales and Yorkshire. All she had was her large rented house, her faith and her memories.

152

COBWEBS AND CANDLELIGHT

I WOULD be woken up by a bang on the bedroom wall connecting with the kitchen where Gran was busily preparing breakfast. Reluctantly, I'd tumble from the high bed and cross the sloping floor to the marble-topped washstand where a steaming jug of water was waiting to be tipped into the deep bowl for me to splash around my face. Gran's antique ewer and basin with their matching soapdish had an exotic Chinese pattern.

I'd stand barefoot on the cold lino to brush my teeth with salt – toothpaste was considered a wasteful luxury. While slipping on my clothes I'd glance through the dusty net curtains dotted with dead flies into the street below. Mrs Bourner, the watch mender's wife, was polishing her doorstep with a pumice stone; Mrs Gadd, the blind chef's wife, was choosing vegetables from the delivery farmcart.

Already there was tremendous activity in this bustling stretch of the boatmen's quarter. Abel's, the boatbuilders, directly opposite, had commandeered strong labourers to steer a newly-built craft along the narrow streets and around the sharp corners on to our steep, shingle beach. There would be a celebration launch. Hats raised and loud cheers.

A red-and-white chequered tablecloth would be laid on the table placed between two windows in the adjoining sitting room. I'd climb on to the hard,

153

varnished, straight-backed chair and patiently wait for my breakfast. Eventually Gran would appear from the long passage balancing a heavy brown teapot with a plate of Hovis bread and butter. My place would be neatly set with a glazed eggcup in the shape of a cockerel and an apostle teaspoon – but where was the egg?

Deftly, Gran produced one from the pocket of her floral pinafore: hot, cracked and steaming, a feather still stuck to its mottled brown shell indicating another supreme effort by her solitary hen which she regarded as a pet! Gran would join me for breakfast, first saying grace as was her custom before eating any meal whether alone or in company:

> *Be present at our table, Lord,*
> *Be here and everywhere adored.*
> *Thy creatures bless. And grant that we*
> *May feast in Paradise with Thee.*

Every summer holiday and most weekends of my childhood I'd stay with Gran in her rambling Georgian house, Redan. This historic building, with its back to the seafront, had once sheltered Nelson's wounded officers after his disastrous Battle of Boulogne in 1801. Although directly in the line of fire from the coastal guns it had survived unscathed during the Second World War.

Gran lived alone in this grand house and paid a pittance rent, which was fortunate since she struggled to survive on her modest state pension. There was a great deal of poverty generally after the war, most noticeably in the North End of Deal. Indeed Gran's life style changed hardly at all from the 1950s until the mid 1970s when she died.

My visits immediately transported me back to the period between the wars and sometimes even farther to the late Victorian period when Gran was a girl. Redan was sparsely furnished and most rooms were stark and cold, particularly in the early afternoon when the sun moved round from east to west and the whole house was in shadow. But when Gran was there, I seem to remember, it was always sunny.

Gran's kitchen was a period piece. A single bulb minus its shade illuminated the centre of the room but that was the extent of her electrical appliances. There was a white stone sink with an enamel washing up bowl in which she piled all the dirty crockery. A kettle needed to be boiled before she could start washing up so there was no topping up with fresh hot water. Underneath the wooden draining board was a curtain modestly concealing materials for household cleansing – Harpic, Dettol, Rinso. A large built-in pine cupboard in a recess held a variety of antique kitchen equipment – a wooden rolling pin, an iron mincer, pottery mixing bowls and tin jelly moulds.

A wooden rocking chair stood beside an enormous kitchen range surrounded

154

by pine cupboards one of which formerly served for keeping blocks of salt dry. I loved the surprise of the winter mornings when Gran had lit the range with coal collected from the beach. I would sit on a wooden milking stool making pictures in the flames, the kettle steaming on the hob. The smell of sausages and bacon and bubble and squeak sizzling in a large frying pan was heavenly! There was an oven at the side for roasting joints but since Gran was too poor to afford expensive meats this was rarely used. In summer when there was no fire it served the opposite purpose of keeping butter cool. At such times you could look up the twisting brick chimney to the open sky and see

the iron rungs where the chimney boys once climbed.

Gran's kitchen was spacious but it held the minimum of furniture. There were two or three bentwood chairs, a rectangular deal table and, in later years, a temperamental gas cooker which she never quite got the hang of. A strip of flypaper  soaked in arsenic spiralled from the ceiling; a pictorial calendar showing a country garden hung by the fire and a pokerwork picture of a laden fishing boat optimistically promised 'The Lord will provide'.

A large copper stood by the sink and this was filled once a fortnight with cold water by means of a hose. There was then all the bother of lighting the gas from underneath which proved a great difficulty for an elderly woman. The soaking garments were prodded with wooden tongs and swished about with a copper dolly while detergent frothed and steam rose from the lid as the garments bubbled and boiled. Afterwards the tangled clothes were emptied into an enamel bowl and piled high into the stone sink. Dismayed, I'd watch as Gran rolled up her sleeves and her arthritic hands wrung out all the water. A hard life.

Later in the week Gran did the ironing. First she spread a thick woollen blanket over the surface of the kitchen table and on this she carefully laid the item to be ironed. She worked two flat irons in tandem – one was heating on the range while she was ironing with the other – mindful to clutch the handles with a pressing cloth for they were stinging hot. She pressed every article from the centre outwards until they were crisp and dry. Freshly ironed garments were then folded over a wooden frame which by means of a pulley was sent up to the ceiling where they hung like bunting at a regatta.

It seems strange now to recall that Gran's kitchen also doubled as a bathroom. Along one entire wall was a deep porcelain bath covered by a wooden lid on which were piled old newspapers and shopping baskets. The bath lacked taps since, as I have said, there was no running hot water.

When a bath was required Gran laboriously ladled warm water from the
steaming copper. It took hours. Task
complete, she firmly shut the door and
disappeared to disrobe amidst clouds of
steam. Bathtime for Gran was infre-
quent and a Very Private Occasion.

Once a week Gran would clean the
house from top to bottom. There was a
minimum of dusting since Gran pos-
sessed few ornaments although I used to admire her rose bowl in carnival
glass and earthenware jug filled with Chinese lanterns and silvery honesty.
While she relentlessly rolled the Ewbank carpet sweeper backwards and forwards across the drugget in the hall I was entrusted with the task of cobweb-
bing. A joyous occasion!

I would step purposely on to the wide landing armed with a cobweb broom.
This consisted of a long bamboo pole to which was attached a miniature
brush. I had to reach with it into the corners of the high ceiling strung with
necklaces of cobwebs. The pole was springy and my aim was precarious but
Gran never once complained when I knocked a picture or pinged a lamp. If

you constantly twisted and turned the broom you
could make a giant stick of candyfloss. Today I'm
dismayed when my cleaner reaches on a chair and
deftly flicks the cobwebs with a duster for they are
such a tangible reminder of my childhood.

Gran would sometimes earn extra money by skivy-
ing. She worked long hours for a certain Mrs
Parsons – a parsimonious woman who spent most of
her life on business in London. I never met her but I
instinctively disliked her for making Gran work so
hard and so long for such little remuneration.
Occasionally I accompanied Gran to this invisible
lady's timber clad cottage on the seafront. There was
a long, dark passage with countless rooms leading
off where hidden clocks chimed dolefully. Miles of
carpeted stairs zigzagged to the upper rooms which
Gran attacked with stiff brush and dustpan, mop and
sweeper.

During the summer Mrs Parsons rented out her seaside cottage. One kindly gentleman had the intrigu-

ing hobby of casting lead soldiers. He presented one to me – a buglar on horseback – which I watched him paint by hand. Wisely, my parents snatched it from me the moment I returned home because the lead was poisonous. Doubtless there would have been a few tears.

Most Saturdays I was entrusted with a trillion errands. One was to collect a gallon of paraffin from the hardware store in the High Street for Gran's precarious heater. A silver florin secreted in my mitten, I swung the battered can which knocked against my knees as I skipped along the cracked pavement. 'Tread on a line, your mother is blind.'

The Dustpan Stores ('Established since the Flood') was a massive hardware shop distinguished by its hideous red dustpan sign displayed over the entrance. Similar emblems appeared in mosaic on the floor as you entered this cavernous store. The interior was dark and dismal and smelled of household cleansers – beeswax polish, moth balls, flyspray, disinfectant. Mops, brooms, hoes and rakes hung from the low beamed ceiling; sacks of seed potatoes and compost rose from the floor. Stalactites and stalagmites.

A sharp, shrivelled woman disappeared along a narrow corridor lined with tiny drawers full of screws and nuts and bolts to fill my can with Esso Blue. Now both hands were required to clutch the can, its screw top oily, as I struggled homewards. Gran sometimes cooked a simple lunch over the newly filled oil stove which perked into life. We sat and ate in silent intimacy.

Afterwards Gran would pull up one of the deep leather armchairs close to the fire in her sitting room and peruse yesterday's *Daily Telegraph* courtesy of a neighbour. I always considered this a highly intellectual journal but Gran, who Valued Education Highly, read every word. Once finished, she would fold the paper in half and place it over her head to blank out the daylight and retire to the Land of Nod. An alternative route to slumber was via forty winks.

While she dozed I would tip the contents of her button box – a Rowntree's cocoa tin – into my lap and sort the articles by shape, style and texture; enamel, brass, bone, plastic, leather, mother-of-pearl. I'd watch fascinated as the

paper rose and fell to Gran's breathing which grew louder and LOUDER until finally – with a volcanic snort – she woke herself up.

'Gran, tell me a story!' Perhaps this was a moment she dreaded for she was by no means an imaginative person. After a deep breath she would begin hesitantly: 'A rabbit was walking down the lane when he met a badger and the two friends walked on further until they met a hedgehog . . .' Invariably, Gran's literary creations were interminable rambles through the countryside so I would dive in to the rescue. 'Remind me about when you were young.' Here we were on more certain ground. Swiftly she flew me back on her magic carpet of memories to the turn of the century and mesmerise me with wonderful tales of her childhood.

Gran hailed from Goldthorpe, a village near Barnsley in South Yorkshire. She was a sickly child, the youngest in a large family, so she often missed her schooling even when her mother could afford the penny fee for tuition. She was so far behind with her lessons that the teacher often made her wear in disgrace the conical dunce's cap. One day a fair arrived in the village. Gran waited until her brothers and sisters had left for school before she ventured out to explore.

Suddenly she was seized by a band of gypsies who carried her off to their caravan. They had been mesmerised by the long red hair that hung down her back. Apparently, they were going to cut it off and turn in into wigs for sale to the gentry at the fair. Luckily, one of her brothers, Sidney, raised the alarm and she was rescued ' . . . in the very nick of time'.

An even more romantic tale touched upon events in history. Gran's maiden name was Trippiear and her French ancestors had been tailors to the aristocracy during the French Revolution. A certain James Trippiear narrowly escaped the guillotine by fleeing to the coast of France and rowing across the English Channel in an open boat. Eventually he settled with his family in the north of England ' . . . where there are Trippiears who are tailors to this day'. Majestically, Gran would fold her arms in triumph.

At other times I would be allowed to explore her cupboards. These were real treasure troves. A large collection of items related to her childhood: a shove ha'penny board, a home made bagatelle; an iron hoop, a writing slate, propelling pencils, a spinning top, glass marbles, wooden skittles and Indian clubs which she continued even in old age to swing precariously for exercise. There was also an assortment of gold rimmed spectacles Gran was collecting to send to missionaries for distribution among the natives in Africa.

Tucked into one enormous cupboard was a horn gramophone with a selection of 78rpm records. Favourites were Eartha Kitt singing An Old Fashioned Millionaire, and King George V addressing children on Empire Day. When the horn became battered and the supply of needles dented I turned the turntable into a roundabout. A friend and I held hands and whizzed round for hours until we broke the machine completely. Its amazing what grans let kids get away with.

By now it would be time for tea. Gran's teas were extraordinary. Every weekday round about four o'clock she would carefully lay the table in the sitting room – none of the china matched – for three or four people. There was a mound of huffkins, a bowl of green salad and perhaps a thin jam sponge but little else. Then, one by one, her friends would arrive: Mrs Barnes with a quarter of best ham, Mrs Gadd with a cake she had just baked and little Mrs Moore with some homegrown tomatoes. None of her guests had been invited: they just happened to be in the town and called in for tea. And there they sat - still wearing their hats - in that sunny room and reminisced and laughed until the tears ran down their rosy cheeks.

In later years these wonderful companions still struggled up those steep stairs for Gran's tea parties, sure of their welcome.

Few of Gran's contemporaries could read or write. This could be a cause of further merriment. Once one old lady brought round a 'birthday' card she had purchased and, being illiterate she wanted Gran to sign it on her behalf. Gran dissolved in tears of mirth. In florid letters it said: 'IN DEEPEST SYMPATHY'. The lady had obviously been smitten by the arrangement of white lilies but had not connected the card with bereavement!

In the evenings Gran would sit and read for hours, mainly history or biography, never crime nor romance. An uneducated woman, she revelled in royal lives and knew the intimate details of all the kings and their mistresses. There was always a hunt for her reading glasses which would generally be rescued from the sides of her armchair along with stray Rennie indigestion tablets, buttons, coins, tracts and sweet papers. Her favourite sweets were Chlorodines – chloroform-flavoured brown lozenges carved like tombstones. Alternative confectionery was winter mixture, acid drops, violet cachous or mint imperials which she munched and crunched while attending the courts of Good Queen Bess or Merry King Charles.

Old fashioned smells pervaded the rooms. Gran's handkerchiefs were daubed with camphor or eucalyptus oil whenever a cold threatened. In summer she dabbed cool lavender or rose water on her wrists and behind her ears. Drawers reeked of mothballs to protect her clothes. Friends might bring her lily-of-the-valley or wild violets that wilted in vases on the sideboard.

Many of her friends were named after flowers, which was a quaint Victorian fashion. They were Lily, Iris, Rose and Violet. A few of her friends terrified me. Belle Wratten sat bolt upright dressed in sombre mourning clothes (for her late, lamented husband) as she thumped mournful ballads on the ivory keys of her ancient upright piano. Waxy candles in polished brass sconces resembled shrouds in coffins as they jerked their ghostly dance of death. Old Mrs Hollins, bent double with arthritis, spoke in a high pitched squeaky voice. She was a dear, sweet lady but I was petrified when left alone with her in her damp, dismal parlour. She reminded me of a witch as she poked the fire of her range with her white bony fingers.

Best friend of all was Mrs Barnes, a Lancashire lady, bubbling over with fun and energy. She was constantly travelling abroad for long holidays although well into her seventies. On one occasion, finding herself at the gates of a grand mansion on the Isle of Capri, she rang the garden bell and was invited in to take tea with the great Gracie Fields. She had a gentleman friend, a certain Mr Spooner, whose spasmodic visits were heralded by the application of thick make-up, much to the amusement of Gran. Mrs Barnes had a television in her sitting room, a tall wooden box with a minute bulbous green screen concealed by a curtain. I never once saw it working so I presumed she was ashamed of it and wanted to keep it a secret – like her weekend lover.

Occasionally Gran wrote letters. She loved receiving replies from friends and relatives, particularly those who had emigrated to New Zealand. Sadly, in later years, these cards and letters were bordered in black indicating that an acquaintance had died. Gran scorned Biros but preferred a fountain pen filled with jet black ink. She wrote in the laborious, old-fashioned copperplate style. Always she used Woolworth's cheap, lined, blue writing paper and envelopes and bought one stamp at a time. To save paper she wrote on both sides. Rather than begin a new sheet she would turn the page and write around the extreme edge of all four sides – like a Victorian 'crossed' letter – before blotting it and sealing it in the flimsy envelope with evident satisfaction.

Television arrived courtesy of Rediffusion. This was a cheap method of viewing since, for a weekly rental, television was relayed via cable to a hired set. It had a further advantage in that London ITV, which commenced in 1955, could be received ahead of Southern Television. Stations were selected by means of a dial affixed to the wall and the quality of the sound was so good that people often hired Rediffusion just to listen to the radio. Folk without a television could then listen to the programmes without viewing, which was a rather strange experience. Gran was highly critical of all she viewed and sent a barrage of complaining letters (often concerning the Independent channel) to BBC Television Centre. One of my last memories of her is of watching Churchill's funeral one afternoon in the mid 1960s. All the cranes dipped in Docklands as the funeral launch passed downstream along the River Thames. Gran's comment, however, was far from sentimental: 'That old warmonger!' But then during the war she had lost her only son in action in Burma. And she never could forget that Churchill set the troops against the miners during their strike for better working conditions in the 1920s.

Gran was often outspoken on the most surprising subjects. Although she was born in the latter part of Queen Victoria's reign she regarded herself as being a true Edwardian, which meant politics, money and even sex were fair topics for conversation. Victoria she dismissed as having 'done nothing for her people'.

Gran was even incensed when Noel Coward introduced a variety show on television on the occasion of the Queen Mother's sixtieth birthday. Perhaps, unwisely, he began his fawning speech: 'We who love our country so much . . .' Gran snapped the television off with the tart comment: 'So much you live abroad to avoid paying our taxes!'

Gran repeated a variety of aphorisms which have since disappeared from general conversation. 'Mutton dressed as lamb' effectively dismissed an older woman attired in a style too youthful for her age, while another woman considered to be far too forward in that direction would be condemned as having 'all the goods in the shop window'. 'Look after the pennies and the pounds will look after themselves' seemed to be a practical maxim for a person in her own impoverished state, but a completely worthless item might be dismissed as 'not worth a brass farthing' (a reference to Victorian tradesmen's tokens). Harking back to military life during recent hostilities there were the phrases 'swear like a trooper', 'soldiering on' or describing anyone who was accident prone as being 'in the wars'.

A woman who thought too highly of herself was considered to be the 'bees knees' or 'cat's

162

whiskers' and a haughty woman was deemed a 'begum' or a 'tartar'. The worst insult Gran might hurl at anyone was that they had treated her 'shoddily', a term derived undoubtedly from her early life in the cotton mills of Manchester. Shoddy referred to inferior cloth. Basically, Gran was a peaceful person who offered this wise advice for settling any dispute: 'Least said, soonest mended'.

One thing I now find quite disturbing was Gran's attitude regarding coloured people. She was a kindly lady, particularly towards animals, and had taken in two stray cats. One was pure black so she called it Nigger. This was meant as a term of endearment but even so it would never be tolerated nowadays. Gran also gave me a cast-iron nigger bank to encourage me to save. It was formed in the shape of a negro's head. You placed a coin in its outstretched palm and when you pressed a switch at the rear it swallowed the money – eyes raised in a comical manner.

Not all Grans room's were electrified. There was a varied source of lighting – candles, torches and oil lamps (one of which had a rich ruby bowl) that came into their own during the power strikes of the early 1970s. Late at night Gran would stand on a chair to light the gas lamp in the centre of the landing with a wax taper. After a long struggle with various chains and pulleys the lamp would reluctantly hiss and sputter into life to give a comforting milky glow. Afterwards Gran would hold up photographs of departed members of her family in silver frames containing snippets of their hair which stood in rows on the heavily ornate sideboard and . . . she never saw me looking . . . kiss each one in turn goodnight.

Time for bed. Gran always let me stay up late and left it until I was well and truly tired before I made for our bedroom. In any case she would be reading her Bible in the sitting room until well past midnight. 'Thy word is a lamp unto my feet, and a light unto my path.' I changed into pyjamas, checked that the po was in position and climbed on to the high double bed where I slept

163

beside Gran. The twin gas sconces threw shadows which danced a hornpipe on the wall above the empty cast iron fire grate.

Her large bedroom had a sloping floor covered with cheap linoleum. There was a large walk-in closet where gentleman powdered their wigs in Georgian times, now piled high with junk. The room was spotlessly clean and tidy although again there was little furniture – a treadle sewing machine, a chest of sticky drawers, an enormous wardrobe with a long foxed mirror. A framed picture of Gentle Jesus – meek and mild – cradling all the children of the world hung on one wall.

The dressing table had a swivel oval mirror which reflected the immense gaslit room. The surface was protected by an applique runner on top of which was a pretty pink porcelain dressing table set – cream jar, pin tray, ring tree, hair tidy, hatpin holder, candlestick. In the top drawer were two precious pieces of jewellery, a gilt dove bearing an olive leaf with a pin attached to a chain, and a garnet necklace. They had both belonged to her mother.

Ours was an Edwardian mahogany bed inlaid with marquetry of sprigs of flowers and lovers bows on its curved head. There was a thin mattress on top

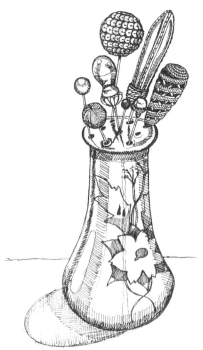

of the wire mesh, and feather bolsters, plump pillows and a pink eiderdown. On a card table within reach was a candle in an enamel save-all, a jug of water capped with a glass and a dish of butter cubes sprinkled with sugar to soothe my throat whenever I had a cough.

Gran's remedies were primitive yet effective. Wasp stings were daubed with vinegar which immediately took away the pain; mouth ulcers were sprinkled with salt that hurt terribly but cured the sore. Mild eye complaints were treated with boracic crystals diluted in water and applied with a tiny blue glass eyebath shaped like an eggcup. Tummy aches were dealt with promptly by mixing ground ginger with warm water, a concoction which tasted vile but was instantly soothing.

Gran would creep into bed much later. I pretended to be asleep but I watched her tiptoe across the sloping floor, struggle

164

to undo her corsets in the dark and pull on a flannel nightdress. Then she would untie her bun so that her hair –once fiery red, now cloudy grey – fell in long folds down her stooped back. She would pull down the blinds (blackout curtains which had survived the war) and blow out the candle. As we lay silently side-by-side we could hear every whispered word from passers-by echoing round Middle Street.

Orange flames from the gas jets hissed and jigged in their cracked glass shades over the dusty mantelpiece tempting menacing ghosts from their lair: Lord Nelson ducked underneath the washstand . . . smugglers bobbed behind the dressing table . . . Crimean troops stormed the chest of drawers . . . and the guillotine blade sliced above my bedhead narrowly missing the bolster. Warm and cossetted, I slid beneath the blankets and drifted off to sleep as these shadows from the past once more claimed for themselves that dark, mysterious house.

SECRETS AND SURPRISES

THIS year, next year, sometime, never . . . Everything in the 1950s followed a strict pattern. Unhurried, we were content to let matters run their
due course. 'Whatever will be will be,' ran the lyrics of a popular song by
Doris Day. 'Que sera, sera.' Each new change of season brought different
treats but nothing was over commercialised. Spring flowers were not available
at the florists in the autumn; playground games arrived in rotation throughout the year and Easter eggs did not appear in the shops immediately after
Christmas.

Pantomime had long seasons and tended to run for several winter months in
large towns and cities. Pop stars began to make their appearance in lead roles
and male principal boys started to emerge. Canterbury's Marlowe Theatre presented traditional Christmas pantomime but, lacking transport, it was difficult
for our family to attend. One year kind neighbours included me in their party
and I watched a spectacular production of Jack and the Beanstalk. Who the
stars were I cannot recall but the thrill of the songs, dances, special effects and
comic turns made me over excited so that for weeks afterwards I relived the
action and could hardly sleep.

My first visit to a proper play, however, was almost my last. Father had taken
the family by train to stay with his sisters in Derby. Confident we would arrive
by mid-afternoon, they had booked seats at the theatre for that same evening.
We arrived late and found our tickets pinned to the front door so, dumping our
luggage in the coal shed, we made our way to The Playhouse.

166

The first act was drawing to a close but Mum,
Dad and I were ushered into the auditorium where
we squeezed along the row to three vacant tip-up
seats. People sat in total darkness and stared ahead at a brightly lit stage in the
far distance. There a middle-aged man dipped his feet into a mustard bath,
slowly dried them with a towel and began to cut his toenails with scissors. At
every snip the audience roared with laughter. What happened next I never
knew because, overcome with tiredness, I fell asleep before the interval.
Thereafter when friends suggested a trip to the theatre I declined without hesi-
tation. Why anyone would want to sit in a darkened room full of strangers
simply to watch a man bathe his feet baffled me!

Our holiday in Derby introduced me to a novel form of transport. Trolley
buses. They were painted in a dark green livery and the double seats were
upholstered in brown leatherette with chrome frames. I must have been quite
young when I first travelled on one because my feet never reached the floor.
For sure I sat up the front so I could watch the driver. It was a smooth, silent
ride. The uniformed conductor
tore our tickets from a roll and
punched the correct fare with his
machine slung over his shoulder.
Ping! When I looked out of the
window I could see the driver of
a stationary trolley bus reach for
his long bamboo stick stowed
under his vehicle and attach the
poles that had come adrift to the
overhead conductor wires. There
were a great many notices displayed inside our trolley bus
including one forbidding spitting, which I assumed to be a
regional pastime.

Further family outings in Derby
included a visit to the cattle market, a picnic in the arboretum
and a conducted tour of the
Crown Derby china factory.
Mother greatly admired the intri-
cate garlands of flowers on the
exquisite china. I watched

167

enchanted as one young artist painted a delicate pattern of fruit on to a shallow dish before it was fired. She gave me one of the cherries she was copying. I have never forgotten her.

Mother's Day was treated almost as a religious ceremony. My mother dutifully stayed in bed until tea was brought to her on a tray and breakfast was ready to be served in the kitchen. She expressed delight with my gift – an apple corer or a pastry brush – bought with my own pocket money from Woolworth's. She would insist on attending morning service at Sunday School and sat at the back with all the other mums while we sang sentimental hymns and listened to a confusing address from which we gathered that Mothering Sunday really had nothing to do with either mothers or religion. Nevertheless the children were primed to offer their token gifts of posies and tracts which the village mothers returned with hugs and kisses. After this rare show of affection we returned home in embarrassed silence to a meal of tough beef which father had cooked as his contribution to the occasion.

Shrove Tuesday always came as a pleasant surprise. I'd arrive home from school at lunchtime to find Gran whipping up batter in a pudding basin. Generally she made scrumptious pancakes, wafer thin, buttery and with a squeeze of lemon. She prided herself in tossing pancakes from the frying pan but once, forgetting our prefab had a low roof, I watched her mount a chair and scrape the debris from the kitchen ceiling.

Easter was a solemn affair with the emphasis firmly on religion. Shops were closed on Good Friday and there was little socialising over the weekend. Home made cards were handed around but chocolate eggs were hidden away until Easter Sunday. Gran and I would go to chapel while Mum and Dad prepared lunch, and afterwards we might go for a walk in the country as a family. On Easter Monday Dad watched sport on television. Wrapped in a warm duffel coat I ventured out

into the avenue hoping my mates would join me in a game of footie.

April Fools' Day was looked forward to and planned with perfect precision. The pranks

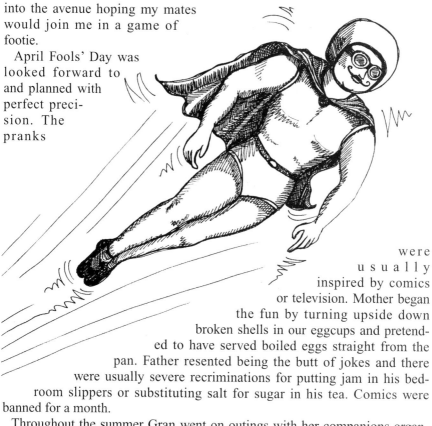

were usually inspired by comics or television. Mother began the fun by turning upside down broken shells in our eggcups and pretended to have served boiled eggs straight from the pan. Father resented being the butt of jokes and there were usually severe recriminations for putting jam in his bedroom slippers or substituting salt for sugar in his tea. Comics were banned for a month.

Throughout the summer Gran went on outings with her companions organised by the numerous chapels she attended. As Gran grew older Mum used to escort her to the coach station. Gran violently stabbed a hatpin into her beret and prepared for action. It was like a reunion of the Home Guard or a reenactment of the Battle of Britain. Armed with walking sticks for rifles and handbags for grenades these old girls fought viciously for the front seat near the driver. Poor Mum was horrified by the ferocity occasioned by these church outings.

Whatever the destination the church ladies made first for the tea rooms and then for the souvenir shops to stock up on sweets and novelties. When I was young I used to accompany Gran by taking my stool to ride free in the centre aisle of the coach. On the way home I crept along to the back seat where the row of fat jolly ladies sucked rock, waved to all the men they passed and sang music hall songs: 'Daisy, Daisy, give us your answer, do'.

169

At midsummer, the mammoth blue and white striped tent of Billy Smart's Circus pitched on Victoria Park. The elephants were led down in procession to bathe in the sea and the showgirls proved mindful of their devotions by attending the local church. A ring of cages containing wild beasts formed a travelling menagerie and there was a grand parade of animal performers through the town. Posters on every lamp post and tree promised a carnival of animals, including snakes and crocodiles.

Neighbours again decided to treat me so I went with an aunt and uncle and their young family from the prefabs to watch the thrilling spectacle. The ringmaster dressed in his scarlet coat and top hat cracked his whip to usher each act in turn into the cramped sawdust ring. There were plumed ponies, performing seals, a chimps' tea party and a boxing kangaroo. Tigers jumped reluctantly through fiery hoops; a lion tamer put his head in a lion's mouth and an elephant tiptoed delicately over a lady who lay on the floor. There were knife throwers, stilt walkers and clowns driving an exploding automobile.

At the dizzy heights athletic youths attired in leopard skins somersaulted from trapezes and a beautiful maiden spun from a rope suspended from the ceiling. First by her hair and then by her teeth. A white faced clown with a striped umbrella attempted to walk the high wire and just as he reached one end he wobbled and ran in terror the whole way back! There was tremendous excitement when a man was shot from a cannon. Wooooow! A desultory act

170

with performing poodles replaced the advertised snakes and crocodiles but we hardly felt cheated as, before the days of animal rights, we had revelled in an afternoon of harmless fun.

Every summer Gran had a visitor who stayed a fortnight for bed and breakfast. Mrs Gooding was a plump, jovial lady with wobbly nicotine-stained teeth and, to a child, tremendous company. She was a farmer's wife from Surrey and her chief delight was to fish from Deal pier. What she caught was served for breakfast so Gran found her a most welcome guest.

One year, in return, Mrs Gooding offered for my family to visit her farm in Godalming. This proved to be a novel experience. The remote farm was set at the bottom of a valley miles from anywhere and the domestic animals included bed bugs and kitchen cockroaches. There was no electricity, no gas, no running water, no inside toilets . . . The farmyard extended into the kitchen and even there the mud was inches deep.

The Goodings had a *laissez faire* attitude to life. Their masculine daughter, Jenny, made model aeroplanes which hung from the low beams of her bedroom. As a youngster I was allowed to steer the tractor across the fields and as a special treat I led the prize bull into the yard by tugging the rope attached to a ring in its nose. Mother panicked and cut the visit short – our only true family holiday.

Summer holidays lingered on and on . . . and there seemed to be endless sunshine. As children we were generally left to amuse ourselves around the prefabs. Our gang regarded family holidays as an unwelcome intrusion. Coach trips were tolerated since they were of short duration. There was a full day excursion to Maidstone Zoo (in a decidedly tatty state) and an afternoon drive round the bays of Kent (rather desultory since they all looked alike).

Other times my family explored Bobby's department store in Folkestone (where you could slide down the polished wooden banisters) and Lyon's Corner House in Canterbury (where we were served by the famous nippy waitresses). One memorable excursion was a review of the fleet on one of the famous Navy Days at Chatham.

Mystery trips were popular when the destination was concealed but usually consisted of a drive through the Alkham Valley with tea in the old worlde village of Elham. Whatever the trip, the driver generally managed to return at dusk via Ramsgate Harbour to admire the coloured lights hidden in the rocks depicting enchanting scenes of fairyland. An illusion of movement was cleverly created whereby clowns rode bicycles and butterflies flapped their wings.

A visit to the newly opened

Model Village at Ramsgate was a wonderful treat. Paths meandered through woodland and bridges lifted you over streams stocked with large goldfish. I was almost as high as the houses and could peer into the hospital ward to watch an operation in the theatre; look into the church porch where a wedding ceremony was in progress and peep into the castle where prisoners were chained in the dungeons. There was a grand hotel with sunbathers beside the pool, a petrol station with saloon cars in the showroom, a public school with a football match played on its sports field and a zoo where a woman was frantically trying to rescue her son who had tumbled into the lion pit! The school bell sounded, the church organ played, the sweeps of the windmill spun round and the cliff lift ascended and descended like the real one at Folkestone.

A miniature steam train followed the banks of the river before disappearing into a dark tunnel. There was a touch of humour in the shop signs: Blood and Thunda, booksellers, Block and Tackle, ship's chandlers, Banger and Smash, garage.

Over the years the model village has acquired a true period feel. I have an inevitable sense of nostalgia whenever I return and now tower over the slightly dilapidated miniscule village that appeared so modern in the post-war era of my youth.

One warm day my entire family decided to visit Margate and picnic on the crowded cloying sands. The pleasures of the seaside for a boy who couldn't swim and hated sunbathing were limited so my attention strayed to the gaudy row of shops selling novelty rock and forbidden amusement arcades. I loved the penny-in-the-slot machines whose jerky automata featured negro minstrels, a laughing sailor or a haunted churchyard where graves opened to reveal ghosts and skeletons.

A waxworks museum, mercifully long forgotten, was tucked into the cliffs. It boasted a Chamber of Horrors, the very name of which intrigued me so I pleaded to be treated to this hidden, hideous spectacle. 'I won't be scared, I promise. Honestly, I won't be scared. Nothing scares me, Mum. Please.' Gran, unwisely, succumbed to my emotional blackmail and led me by the hand into the darkened, curtained interior.

There, as large as death, paraded all the criminals of the past – Crippen, Haigh, Jack the Ripper, whose glassy eyes stared back as if to say: 'You're next!' There was Smith disposing of his naked bride in an overflowing bath and Christie pasting up the wallpaper in the kitchen to conceal his latest victim. The most frightening display was a replica of 'The Thing', a shapeless monster washed up on the beach sometime, somewhere . . . For months afterwards these terrifying effigies worked on my imagination and I could not sleep for fear that someone would creep into my bedroom and poison my glass of water for the night.

Margate's Dreamland was a must. We joined the jostling crowds slipping down the dark incline alongside the Art Deco cinema on the seafront with the word DREAMLAND emblazoned on its tall, angular tower. We passed under the grotesque giant snailman whose perverse and cruel smile warned of the Wages of Sin. Beyond lay Vanity Fair!

American GIs stationed at nearby Manston, and their temporary sweethearts who worked at local factories, flocked to this famous fairground in the immediate post-war period. There were a million pleasures to be experienced: the roller coaster, racing cars, cash bingo, zoo land, the enormous skywheel combining two big wheels in one and the scenic railway which remains one of the few wooden gravity rides in Europe.

The Caterpillar was an amusing ride to watch. Couples squashed into the twin seats of a sprawling train whose huge wheels sped round an undulating circular track. Once the ride had attained maximum speed an enormous green hood snapped into position overhead plunging the riders into darkness. Just as suddenly this canvas hood rolled back to reveal courting couples in the act of snogging! Klaxons sounded and a blast of compressed air under the seats lifted girls' skirts over their heads – to the merriment of bystanders.

Mum's favourite ride was the Magic Caves. We sat in large metal tubs that spun along a swift flowing waterway driven by a thunderous waterwheel to experience a sequence of illuminated tableaux concealed in realistic plaster and cement caves: The Ice Cave, The Venetian Cave, The Smugglers' Cave.

Here was my one and only opportunity to watch a flea circus. After paying sixpence, a princely sum, I pushed my way to the front of a cramped and crowded auditorium. A miniature circus ring was laid out in front of the spectators. There was a hushed air of expectation. A presenter took out the fleas with tweezers, one by one, from matchboxes labelled with their stage names, and gently coaxed them into performing amazing tricks. One flea pushed a minute garden roller, another wielded weights while a third rode a bicycle on a tightwire. Admittedly I couldn't actually see any fleas. One Doubting Thomas whispered it was all done by invisible wires and magnets. But I was not convinced.

A final treat before home might be a ride around the car park in a miniature coach. Kids crammed into the tiny seats while the driver steered with his head stuck out through the roof. Towering over Dreamland was the 330ft long replica of the Cunard liner, *Queen Mary*. Cabins built into her twin funnels contained an observation post and a broadcasting studio which played When Day Is Done every night as a signal for the fairground to close.

Hallowe'en was rarely mentioned. Certainly it had not attained the epic proportions it has today under the influence of America where it is actually celebrated. Our interest was artistic rather than supernatural. We might make a Jack o' Lantern by scooping out the pulp from a pumpkin, carving a weird face and inserting a nightlight, or perhaps construct a mobile of witches riding broomsticks around a crescent moon. Nonetheless our gang lost little opportunity for creating mischief and ginger knocking provided a feast of fun. One night we tied string across the streets linking several door knockers so that as the first door was opened to our call it sent a chain of knocks reverberating around the street.

A month before Bonfire Night friends organised themselves into rival gangs of workforces to build fires on scrubland behind the prefabs. Tortuously, molehills became mountains with planks and branches, newspaper bundles and cardboard boxes. Prams and go-carts were requisitioned for the collection of broken cupboards, discarded cots, battered chairs, three legged tables. Each night the timber pyramids would be covered with tarpaulin against the ele-

175

ments and jealously guarded by their owners who kept watch by torchlight from nearby bedroom windows.

Making a Guy Fawkes involved the entire community of children. Torn pillowcases, sacks and stockings were stuffed with paper, straw or sawdust and stitched together in the shape of a figure. Discarded clothing was scrounged to dress the body and a painted mask was tied round the head. Hats, scarves, boots, gloves and spectacles were added to create a realistic effigy. This was then propped inside a pram and wheeled around the streets with the plaintive cry 'Penny for the Guy'. Once we cut corners by disguising Peter Dry as a guy and carried him round our prefabs in an attempt to con coins from our parents. We stopped short of dumping him on the bonfire.

Parents, too, were involved in all the fun. Fireworks provided piece-work for mothers who made casings for the local factory. Astra Fireworks – whose logo was a man made from fireworks – was based at Richborough, near Sandwich. The factory had a peculiar layout consisting of tiny brick sheds where two or three people worked in safety protected by a blast-proof wall. Recently, the site was razed to the ground; it ought, perhaps, to have been preserved as a curiosity.

Firework parties at home tended to be a damp squid. Father hated to see good money go up in smoke. As a toddler I can recall watching our grand display from the kitchen window but when I could be trusted I wandered out into the yard – togged out in warm coat and woolly hat – to hold a sparkler. Once, though, the spectacle was destroyed when a catherine wheel spun into the open box and all our fireworks exploded in an instant.

Each year Gran would insist on producing treats for Bonfire Night. She made parkin, which was a sticky cake spiced with ginger, and black treacle toffee baked in a shallow tray which we cracked with one of the miniature hammers that came with slabs of Sharp's toffee. Like geologists. This latter

homemade concoction was responsible for seeing off the last of my milk teeth. In all honesty we found both of Gran's delicacies revolting but it pleased her to revive these traditional treats from her Yorkshire childhood.

Street firework parties, however, were grand social occasions. We danced in the dark around the bonfire and ate baked potatoes roasted in the embers. Dads supervised the fireworks – Brock's or Pain's – firing rockets from milk bottles, dodging exploding jumping jacks and holding huge coloured matches in gloved hands. Roman candles . . . snowstorms . . . silver cascades . . . dive bombers . . . electric squibs . . . witch's cauldrons . . . Mount Vesuvius . . . flaming arrows . . . golden rain . . . And as each firework exploded in colourful cascades there were appreciative cries in unison: 'Ooh! Aaaaah!'

When all seemed to be dying down or burned out there was still the additional thrill of wandering down to the seafront to observe the bonfires on the beach. For weeks these had amassed on the foreshore and each year they seemed to grow bigger and bigger. We wandered along the prom where we were level with the tips of the bonfires to share the heat with the tormented guys. Here was the stolen pleasure of watching other people's firework displays. The police eventually stepped in and restricted first the size and then the number of the bonfires until Deal's tradition of bonfires on the beach passed into history.

Christmas comes but once a year . . . In mid-December there was a desperate hunt for the Christmas decorations. Paper garlands concertinad around the walls and criss-crossed the ceiling of our lounge. These were interspersed by enormous stars, bells and circles. Favourites were the miniature paper Chinese lanterns in pastel shades. We even hung up a sprig of mistletoe although there was nobody much to kiss. Fifties decorations were chunky, gaudy and rather oppressive but I adored them and I wanted them to stay up all year round.

A wobbly crib was placed on the sewing table in one corner and the plaster figures of the Holy Family lovingly laid out on cotton wool snow. Pity that the ancient kings now bore chipped gifts but Baby Jesus looked snug for all that in his cardboard cradle. At least he could reach out and help himself to the bowls of nuts with the awkward nutcrackers, presentation boxes of crystalised fruits, oval cardboard trays of sticky dates with their plastic forks and mandarins seasonally wrapped in soft tissue paper.

Great excitement was assured when at last Father unfolded the artificial Christmas tree stored in a rectangular box tucked in a cupboard for eleven months of the year. Four feet high with green needles attached to a wire frame, it looked like an outsize bottle brush. Each year Father assumed the task of decorating the tree so he would normally invest in a further set of blown glass coloured baubles from Woolworth's. Traditional elements of our family tree included a miniature basket woven from raffia, a pair of glass birds with brush tails and a plastic dolly with rolling eyes which served as a fairy precariously perched on the topmost branch. Plastic icicles, miniature parcels, tinkling bells, strips of tinsel. Lastly the string of coloured lights was wound around like a mummy before the grand switching-on ceremony. The only daunting touch was that Father would allow only flashing lights since he considered this would halve the electricity bill.

Gran, by contrast, preferred a real tree. Invariably this was a short, dumpy, sparse affair plonked in a

178

bucket in a dark recess. Its decorations still reflected wartime austerity – painted pine cones, strings of coloured milk bottle tops, thin wax candles stuck in metal clip-on sconces and a tinsel star instead of a fairy on the top of the tree.

One year she gave a party, the high point of which was a display of indoor fireworks. Once lit, bits of paper twisted into the fantastic shapes – you had to stretch your imagination – of flowers and animals. We tried them only that once because they singed Gran's best tablecloth.

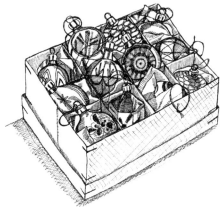

Every evening we went carolling around the avenue. We sang at least two full verses before we dared request any money. 'You knock and I'll ask.' I wrote letters to Santa to post up the chimney but there was great consternation as to whether his reindeers and sleigh could land on our low ribbed prefab roof. We lit the candles of the revolving angel chimes and played, endlessly, Dickie Valentine's 1955 hit Christmas Alphabet:

S is for old Santa who makes every kid his pet.
Be good and he'll bring you everything in his
Christmas ALPHABET!

One Christmas I awoke to find that it had snowed overnight. Deep and crisp and even. Muffled up with coat, scarf and mittens – sniffing Vick and sucking Zubes to ward off colds – I dashed into the avenue to join in a terrific snow-ball fight. We created our own slides and made our own sledges. Fathers quickly knocked up toboggans for rapid rides down the slopes. Susan and John McGrath came over to help build a snowman. While we rolled a giant snowball for a head our parents patted out the body with shovels. Lumps of coal for eyes, a carrot for a nose. A cap, a scarf, a pair of gloves. We even found a pipe to stick in his mouth. Once the thaw set in I watched with dismay, my nose pressed against the prefab window, as he melted and withered away.

Christmas Eve was the most exciting day of the year. Eager with anticipation I joined the noisy crowds in Woolworth's where the shopgirls stood in the centre of the high mahogany counters with sprigs of holly pinned to their white caps. Like boxed Celluloid dolls. Coloured tinsel dropped from the ceiling; glass baubles glittered over the shelves. At dusk the interior of the store was

179

illuminated with fairy lights. Aladdin's cave.

Dad had given me money to buy a present for Mum; Mum had given me money to buy a present for Dad. It was the thought that counted: a waffle iron and a peg bag for mum, a garden gnome and a puncture repair kit for dad. How they would be surprised! For Gran there were bath cubes, a bookmark and Eau de Cologne. These parcels would be packed tight into a sturdy carrier bag with string handles that bit into my hands. Later, Dad, drawing on his shopkeeper's expertise, would help me to wrap the gifts with brown paper, tie them with

coloured twine and seal them with melted wax.

The happiest moment of my childhood was watching Gran struggling with her arthritic hands and diminishing eyesight to wrap her Christmas presents for the family. She sat in her dimly lit but cheerful front room surrounded by cheap gifts and scraps of

coloured paper. When she came to my present I was sent out of the room although she guessed I'd be peeping through the keyhole. After wrapping each item she forced it into one of three old stockings filling out the gaps with little delicacies – toffees, nuts and fruit. There was a tangerine in every toe. If only one could go back in time . . .

On Christmas morning I awoke bright and early to find Santa had not forgotten this small boy. I bounced to the end of the bed, startling Gran who was still asleep in the adjacent twin, to investigate the contents of my pillow case which was stuffed with secrets and surprises. Money may have been in short supply in the early 1950s but my family had saved all year round to ensure plenty of wonderful gifts. Aunts and uncles, neighbours and friends had chosen with care: a brand new pair of roller skates; a china fish money box; a cedarwood pencil case; rolling stock for the railway, glass snowstorms, Noddy soap, suction darts . . . From somewhere there came a remote controlled American car – the controls were battery operated and connected to the vehicle via a thick plastic cable.

My parents gave me their gift separately. One year it was a Mickey Mouse watch by Timex. His white gloved hands pointed to the figures on the dial. Another year it was a Raleigh bicycle with wooden pedals.

I couldn't wait to get out into the avenue where all my mates were already inspecting each other's toys and trying out new bikes and trikes. We'd stay out all Christmas if we could but were generally called in for lunch and The Queen's

181

Speech. Queen Elizabeth made her first televised speech in 1957, an event which happily coincided with my family's first acquiring a 'gogglebox'.

My parents did not hurry to open their presents. Breakfast was attended to; vegetables peeled; the fire got going. But they made the right noises as they unwrapped them carefully, one at a time. Family gifts included a set of three initialled hankies for the top pocket of a blazer and Old Spice after shave for Dad; a sherry set consisting of six tiny tumblers and a matching decanter decorated with playing cards and a box of Bronnley Rose Geranium scented soaps for Mum; a bottle of Devon Violets perfume and a crochet shawl for Gran (which she detested because, she said, it made her look like a grandmother). Mindful of the wartime make-do-and-mend, Gran sat in the corner uncreasing wrapping paper and winding up the discarded string.

The three chefs – Mum, Dad and Gran – worked harmoniously in the kitchen, encouraging rather than criticising, a rare demonstration of peace and goodwill in our family. Chicken was a luxury we could rarely afford and might appear on our table once every two years. Prior to frozen foods poultry had to be ordered from a local farm months in advance. Free range, the meat had a delicious flavour. Tender and juicy. One Christmas Father decided the family deserved a special treat and persuaded Gran to sacrifice her scraggy chicken which had given up laying long ago. So he tempted it into the garden shed. And despatched it.

This seemed to me to be a callous betrayal of trust particularly when I had crept into our coal shed and caught Father attempting to pluck the strangled bird amid a blizzard of feathers. Mum and Gran puzzled over its cooking which took the greater part of Christmas morning. When the belated feast was served I slammed my knife and fork down on to the festive table and ran sobbing into the garden. Mum soon joined me in a flood of tears not so much in sympathy for my passionate display of animal rights but because the meat was tough.

More contentedly I thumbed through my Christmas annuals: Rupert Bear, Tiger Tim or Mabel Lucy Atwell. There might also be a pop-up book or a Christmas card in the form of a record you could actually play on the radiogram – Jingle Bells, White Christmas or Rudolf the Red Nosed Reindeer. Later in the decade there was the rich joy of Christmas television to watch as a family. All our favourite stars would be presenting their party pieces: Carols from Canterbury Cathedral; Chipperfield's Christmas Circus; Christmas Night with the Stars . . . Ecstatically, festive viewing would end with an opera.

Boxing Day was inevitably an anti-climax. The Salvation Army played carols in the avenue but we ignored them when they knocked at the front door for a donation. We felt we had given our fair share to charity. The dustmen had received their Christmas box in the form of a £1 note stuffed in an envelope taped to the bin.

Lunch was cold meat or poultry with pickles after which we finished off the last of the chocolates from the seasonal selection boxes. We might be tempted at last to open the homemade elderberry wine which Gran's neighbour, the watch mender's wife, provided annually in a Daddie's sauce bottle. In the afternoon I played with my new Dinky or Corgi toys while Mum and Dad dozed in front of Grandstand. Steeple chasing at Kempton Park . . . motor racing from Brand's Hatch.

In the evening I gave a hesitant performance of conjuring tricks in pale imitation of television magician David Nixon, or gave a dazzling presentation of my prized Pelham Puppets. Christmas television might include a special variety show with Billy Cotton or The Black and White Minstrels followed by a stilted pantomime starring Arthur Askey or Frankie Howerd. Close down on BBC would be well before midnight even at holiday periods but in any case I would be content to retire early to my little bedroom in the prefab. Happily I would snuggle down beneath the woollen blankets, toast my toes on the hot water bottle, cuddle my battered teddy bear and fall sleep surrounded by so much love.

The author and the illustrators

GREGORY HOLYOAKE is an actor, writer and teacher who lives in a restored smuggler's cottage in Deal, the town where he was born half a century ago.

He trained as a schoolteacher at Culham College, Oxfordshire, where he gained certificates in English and Divinity. He taught for five years in Deal Parochial C of E School, where Jane and Anne were among his first pupils.

As an actor he retrained at Rose Bruford College of Speech and Drama in Sidcup, Kent. He has been acting for more than twenty years in national tours, pantomimes, repertory and repertoire. He specialises in comedy and character acting.

Gregory has been a freelance writer and photographer for some twenty-five years. He is a regular contributor to *Country Life, Country Homes and Interiors, The Illustrated London News, The Lady, This England, Heritage* and *The Evening Standard.*

He is an authority on Kentish subjects and writes monthly for *Kent Life.* His subjects are diverse: Village Schools, Country Garages, Cricket Pavilions, Cottage Gardens, Animal Architecture, Ships' Figureheads, Rural Post Offices, Ice Cream Parlours, Windmills, Scarecrows, Church Bells, Beach Fairs and Character Cats.

Gregory has recently published a biography of the Duke of Wellington as Lord Warden of the Cinque Ports, and is currently working on a photographic book of Kent.

JANE MICHAEL and **ANNE CHURCHILL** are sisters who often work in partnership as illustrators. They were both born in Deal and attended Deal Parochial C of E Primary School before continuing their studies through secondary education – Jane at Folkestone Technical High School; Anne at Dover Grammar School for Girls.

Jane studied for an honours degree in Graphic Design at Maidstone Art College. There she won the British Design Award in 1981. Jane then worked for a publishing company in London before joining a design group in Folkestone. Married to a fireman, Martyn, and the mother of Hannah and Charlie, Jane now works at home as a freelance illustrator and designer. Her interests include interior design, cycling, swimming, cooking and painting watercolours of local views.

Anne joined her sister at Maidstone College of Art and after completing her foundation course she became interested in fashion and textiles and studied textile design at Huddersfield Polytechnic. Later Anne moved to London where she joined the design team of Zandra Rhodes. Anne returned to Deal where she married Simon, a picture framer. They have two boys, Tom and Toby. Her artistic interests include jewellery making, painting murals, tie dying and batik.

When Jane was nine years old her teacher wrote in her school report: 'Shows an artistic flair'. Little did she think that she might be illustrating a book with her younger sister for that same teacher thirty years later!